1 9 JAN 2019

D0653386

Essex County Council

3013021325162 1

Cooking Tonight

Alex
Hollywood

Cooking
Tonight

HODDER &
STOUGHTON

'Page after page of family favourites, not a gram of pretence, just full of unadulterated delicious joy.'
MICHEL ROUX JR

To my husband Paul
and my son Josh
– for you both **X**

CONTENTS

Cooking Tonight

A while ago I came across a box of recipes and magazines belonging to my husband's grandmother, and it made fascinating reading. Weeks' worth of menus mapped out for the family to consume from morning to night: grilled kippers, toast and marmalade for breakfast; stuffed loin of mutton and roast potatoes for lunch, and tuna-stuffed tomatoes followed by coffee layer cake for pudding. Another booklet suggested hot stuffed eggs, boiled fowl with spinach and gooseberry tart with 'mock cream' for a Tuesday meal in September! Reading these made me think of how fiddly and time-consuming dinner preparation must have been for our grandmothers and how lucky we are now to have so many more unusual, colourful ingredients to play with to spice up our meals.

Well times have certainly changed since then and we may be able to source exotic unusual produce all year round but we are also 'time poor' and the question I hear again and again during the week is 'What are you cooking tonight?'. It's the main topic of conversation on my early morning dog walk with friends, it's a question my lovely agent Jan often asks me whenever we speak on the phone and it's the first question my son asks when he gets in the car on the school pick-up run! So this got me thinking. No matter how many cookery books we buy everyone tends to grab the same ingredients for those Monday to Friday meals – chicken, sausages, mince, fish, chops etc. But because we have so little time to plan mid-week, most of us tend to churn out the same dishes again and again and this is when boredom rears its ugly head and cooking becomes a real drag…

So I decided to write a book based on those basics you have already bought with your weekly shop – the chicken, mince, sausages and chops that are always in your fridge and freezer – and create some quick, easy and delicious recipes that can be thrown together and send you a little bit 'off piste' without it costing an arm or a leg. More importantly you can usually do them in super-quick time – or with a little planning you can make those delicious, long, slow 'one-pot wonders' that are ready for you when you want to sit back, relax and enjoy a meal with the people you love!

Many of these recipes use leftovers and they're mostly versatile enough for it not to matter if you don't have all the right ingredients. The book is based on your weekly shop with chapter titles such as Beef, Sausages and All Things Porky, Mince and Meat-free so that you can check your fridge and freezer first, then choose a dish that works around whatever you have to hand. Try my Quick Hungarian Goulash with Paprika for instance which is great for cold wintry weather or my Chipotle Chilli Chicken Bake, perfect for that lone pack of chicken legs or drumsticks. The little Beef Bourguignon Pies are fab for some mid-week 'poshness' and my absolute favourites when you just want a 'little' something special are toasties: the Guinness Toasties with Cheddar, Ham and Mustard are not to be missed and as for the Grilled Sourdough, Chocolate, Brie and Basil – enough said!

Mealtimes should always be when the family can sit together even for a short while to unwind and relax and enjoy good food. So I hope this book will give you new ideas to bring the 'oomph' back into your mid-week cooking!

Bon appétit. X

Tips for Hassle-free Mid-week Cooking

Mid-week cooking can be a challenge, especially if you come home late from work or are stuck on the school run, collecting from 'footie' or tennis practice. Having a well-stocked larder is your back-up: all those herbs, spices and cans can be grabbed at a moment's notice to jazz up a lonely chicken breast or pack of sausages. With a little planning and forethought you can create some delicious and stress-free meals with minimum effort and those dinner plates on your table will be scraped clean! I'm a firm believer in using what you already have and my recipes are straightforward, simple to follow, and packed with flavour. Shortcuts are a must mid-week. Use up that can of custard: who says you have to make your own pastry from scratch? And the Sunday roast beef is epic sliced with leftover vegetables and stuffed into spiced yoghurt wraps for a meal in minutes.

Larder Necessities

I listed many of these in my last book but the same principles apply here so I hope you don't mind a bit of repetition. Anything goes and the more flavours, herbs, spices and cans you have, the more versatile your recipes will be!

CANS

Salmon, tuna, anchovies.

Beans, chickpeas, lentils, peas, sweetcorn, chopped tomatoes, various chillies.

Lots of fruit (peach halves, apricot halves, cherries).

Coconut milk, custard.

BOTTLES

Oils (olive, vegetable, rapeseed, sesame).

Sauces (sweet chilli, oyster, soy, dark and light, Worcestershire, chipotle, smoked chipotle paste).

Vinegars (balsamic, cider, malt, sherry and wine).

JARS

Mayonnaise, mustard (French, English),
sun-dried tomatoes, tomato passata,
jalapeno peppers (and other chillies),
capers, miso pastes.

I also have many small jars of dried herbs
and spices which I use (and replace)
regularly.

Jams, jellies, honey and marmalade.

PACKETS

Flours (plain, self-raising and wholemeal,
cornflour).

Grains (rice, couscous, quinoa, oats).

Pulses (dried beans, lentils, etc).

Microwave lentils/rice.

Nuts and seeds.

Pasta (of all types, long and short).

Dried noodles.

Dried fruits.

Sugar (brown and white).

Chocolate (milk, dark and white).

Buying Sensibly

This book is for you to glance at when you're out of ideas and need some inspiration but the first thing you're going to need to do is shop a little more creatively until you have the basics of a well-stocked larder and freezer. I often buy meat and fresh fish from the reduced aisle and as long as it is labelled clearly and used within freezer guideline times it means I always have something to hand to cook mid-week. I tend to grab things that look interesting: I love spices especially those with Middle-Eastern undertones. So next time you're out stop and take a look in the 'dried' aisle. Grab a couple of bottles of herbs you are not that familiar with, a tin of za'atar – a sesame and thyme mix perfect for grilled meats – or jars of paste such as the Japanese miso, or some 'jerk seasoning' to rub into chicken and bring the Caribbean to your table…

Cooking is a journey – a taste adventure. Just because you are short of time it shouldn't mean you have to skimp on flavour. So if your herb and spice rack is up to date and you have a larder full of goodies to play with, 'the world is your lobster', as my son used to say!

Using Leftovers

As my Twitter followers know I'm big on leftovers. My mother was a war baby and it was dinned into her from an early age to use up everything and what can't be used goes into the freezer. Bones can be frozen to make stock at a later date, meats can be sliced or minced and made into koftas or meatballs, vegetables end up with fragrant yoghurt dips wrapped in tortillas or thrown into omelettes, and cooked pasta ends up in soups, salads and baked with cherry tomatoes and a béchamel sauce for a super quick supper! Make full use of your freezer in the battle against food wastage. Bag up leftover carrots or roast parsnips to freeze -- you've enough for a soup in the making -- turn your stale bread into breadcrumbs bagged and frozen ready to go and even cake finds its way into my freezer ready to be pulled out for a last-minute trifle. Be flexible and creative!

Using Your Freezer

For quick mid-week cooking your freezer is your best friend! Think before you throw any food out: so much of what we waste can be transformed into another dinner from your freezer. My mother hardly ever threw anything away: she always froze any leftover bits and pieces and as if by magic managed to create something delicious from them. These days we tend to throw far more away but with a little careful planning it actually saves you time to freeze and have to hand when you have little time to prepare a dinner.

• Those last few stale slices of bread in the bread bin should be blitzed up or chopped, bagged and popped in the freezer for when you need to quickly make my bread (ciabatta is my favourite) dumplings to bulk up a soup for supper.

• Mashed potato freezes well and is great for my Fiery Pork Cottage Pie!

• Always have a pack of soft tortilla wraps, which make fantastic savoury and sweet meals, and freeze beautifully. See my Pork Burritos with Kidney Beans and Cheese or make my moreish Nutella, Pear and Granola Quesadillas.

• Chop fresh herbs – parsley, tarragon or sage – and mix with seasoned butter. Roll into a sausage shape, wrap in clingfilm, and freeze ready to be brought out to melt on steaks or fish. I also make savoury butters using caramelised shallots, garlic and grated lemon zest.

• Keep boxed cooked rice ready for stir-fries with sliced peppers and beansprouts in bags so you have the makings of an instant meal.

• Using the carcass from a roast chicken make your own stock every once in a while and freeze in ice-cube trays ready to make a quick sauce, gravy or soup.

• Mix flour, sugar, cinnamon and butter, blitz until it becomes a crumble mixture then bag up and freeze along with a bag or box of frozen fruit or berries: fruit crumble pudding in an instant!

• Bananas that are past their best, slice, bag and freeze: they're perfect for smoothies or quick banana flambé puddings.

• Do the same with onions if they are getting a little soft in the vegetable basket. Chop and double bag them ready for the casserole pan.

• Got an open bottle of red wine? Pop it into ice-cube trays to freeze ready for your sauces or red wine and cinnamon poached fruit!

• Double up the ingredients for a long-cooking stew, and use half that day and freeze the other half for a mid-week dinner another time. I sometimes do this on a Saturday when I have more time. But always remember to take it out of the freezer in time for a proper defrost…

Adding Flavour

For fast, mid-week meals packed with a punch, my weapon of choice has to be my rub mixes. Quick to make and easy to store they are the simplest way of injecting mouth-watering flavour into your meat or fish. They are a mix of herbs and spices that can be 'rubbed' into your steak, chops or fillets. Opening a jar of my Greek Island Herb Mix takes me straight back to the beachside taverna in Kefalonia or my Provençal Mix reminds me of long hot summer days with Monique, my French godmother.

I make these rubs up in batches – you simply mix all the ingredients together – and store them, for no longer than three months, in tightly sealed jars in my cool dark larder so they retain as much of their flavour as possible. You can adapt them to your own tastes by adding more or less of each ingredient.

GREEK ISLAND HERB MIX

This is one of my favourite rubs: it reminds me of supper under the vines on a summer's evening… It's perfect for the barbecue too! I like to use it with white fish (see page 156). Try it also with juicy lamb chops with crumbled Feta or chicken drumsticks with toasted pine nuts and a big Greek salad.

2 tsp garlic powder	½ tsp ground nutmeg
4 tsp onion powder	2 tbsp dried oregano
2 tsp ground cinnamon	2 tbsp dried parsley

PROVENÇAL MIX

This Provençal mix uses lavender which is unusual but the mixture is perfect with goat's cheese, its slightly perfumed aroma complementing the tartness of the cheese. Try it with salmon fillets too, baked and served with a squeeze of lemon or grilled chicken with a plate of buttery asparagus. Go easy with it though as it's powerful stuff and remember to buy edible lavender: you can't just rip open your granny's lavender pillow!

1 tsp dried (edible) lavender

1 tbsp dried rosemary

1 tbsp dried sage

1 tbsp dried thyme

ARABIC SPICE MIX

Cardamom, cumin and coriander are exotic flavours reminiscent of souks and bazaars. Lamb is a favourite meat in Arab countries and this mix is great with lamb kebabs (see page 145), but also works a treat in a rich tomato sauce with mini beef meatballs and grilled pittas.

3 cardamom pods

1 tbsp coriander seeds

2 tsp cumin seeds

1 tbsp coarsely ground black pepper

2 tsp fennel seeds

1 tbsp cayenne pepper

Place the cardamom pods in a pestle and mortar. Lightly crush then remove the green husks leaving the black seeds. Add the remaining seeds to the cardamom seeds and grind until you have a coarse powder. Stir in the cayenne. Store as described above.

ITALIAN HERB MIX

When my baker husband isn't there to knock up a fresh dough… I cheat! My ciabatta pizzas on page 216 are super-quick and just as tasty as the real thing especially with the addition of this herb mix. It's also great with pasta sauce and poured over grilled aubergine with melted mozzarella.

1 tbsp dried parsley, finely chopped

1 tbsp dried basil, finely chopped

1 tbsp dried thyme

1 tsp garlic powder

BROWN SUGAR 'N' SPICE MIX

This really is a case of 'sugar 'n' spice and all things nice'. The rich caramel of the dark brown sugar is essential so don't try and substitute white sugar: it just won't be the same. The mix goes perfectly with white meats (wonderful with the southern chicken recipe on page 57) and even salmon but just watch things don't burn. If anything looks like it's on the turn just reduce the heat. Try it too with chops or big king prawns – lush!

50g dark brown sugar

1 tbsp chilli powder

1 tbsp dried oregano

1 tbsp garlic powder

1 tsp fine salt

STEAK RUB

Steaks are the ultimate fast food. They are quick to cook and very little preparation is needed. I like a steak cooked simply with salt and pepper but sometimes a little more thought needs to go into it and that is where my foolproof rub comes in. It just adds a bit of a flavour kick and is brilliant on less tasty steaks. Try it as well on chicken quarters or pork chops on the barbecue.

1 tbsp sweet paprika

2 tbsp dried oregano

1 tbsp ground cumin

1 tbsp sea salt

SPICY FAJITA MIX

Who doesn't like fajitas? They are super-quick and kids love them. Lots of people I talk to buy the pre-made fajita mix for convenience but why not make your own? It's very simple and is perfect with chicken, steak or even minced beef for tacos. Try it on steak, white fish or prawns or even sprinkled on winter roast vegetables.

2 tsp dried oregano

2 tsp smoked paprika

2 tsp onion powder

1 tsp ground cumin

1 tsp garlic powder

1 tsp chilli powder (hot or mild)

½ tsp chilli flakes

CAJUN SPICE MIX

Flavours of the Deep South. Great on pork, fish and chicken. It's punchy, so use with a good squeeze of lemon and it's good to go. Use as much or as little as you like.

2 tsp paprika

½ tsp cayenne pepper

1 tsp garlic powder

2 tsp dried thyme

2 tsp dried oregano

½ tsp ground cumin

½ tsp ground pepper

½ tsp salt

Soup

A soup is often dismissed as too simple a starter or as being unadventurous but in fact soups can be a hearty meal in themselves: you just need a bit of imagination. I am a practical family cook and love making use of leftovers and those solo carrots and softening tomatoes that lurk at the back of the fridge. Soups are the perfect way to use these bits and pieces up and a great way to get the whole family to eat vegetables (as they can be cunningly disguised when puréed or finely chopped). Better still if you make a big batch of soup it freezes perfectly, making a last-minute lunch for when Grandma pops in unexpectedly.

Beef and Tomato Soup

This really is a great hearty soup. It's one of my son's favourites and is often requested when his friends come round for movie night. Prep time is short although it is a long slow cook: you can just leave it on the hob simmering away whilst you put your feet up.

SERVES 4

2 tbsp olive oil
600g stewing steak, cut into 1cm cubes
2 carrots, chopped
1 onion, chopped
1 tsp smoked paprika
1 tsp ground cumin
1 tsp ground coriander
2 x 400g cans chopped tomatoes
1 litre beef stock, plus a little extra
2 tsp dried oregano
salt and freshly ground black pepper

For the tortilla toasts
4 soft tortilla wraps
2 tbsp olive oil

To serve
1 x 150ml pot soured cream
a handful of coriander leaves

Heat the olive oil in a large pan and brown the beef on all sides (you may want to do this in batches). Remove the beef from the pan and set to one side.

Add the carrot and onion to the pan and cook for a couple of minutes then add the spices. Stir well before returning the beef to the pan.

Pour in the tomatoes, stock and oregano. Cover and simmer gently for 2 hours, stirring occasionally, until the meat is tender.

Preheat the oven to 180°C/Gas mark 4.

Brush the tortilla wraps with a little olive oil on both sides. Cut each into eight triangles. Spread the triangles out on a couple of baking trays and bake in the preheated oven for 5–8 minutes until golden brown and crisp. Leave to cool.

Once the meat is tender adjust the consistency by adding more stock so that it is soupy. Season well. Serve in chunky bowls with a spoonful of soured cream, a good scattering of coriander leaves and your tortilla toasts.

Curried Squash Soup with Oozy Mozzarella

This is a really hearty dinner soup and if you serve it with the scones in the recipe on page 26 it's a warming winter filler. It's perfect for a super-speedy meal if you have a pot on the stove ready for dinner-time and both the soup and scones freeze beautifully.

SERVES 2–4

2 tbsp olive oil
1 red onion, roughly chopped
1 tsp ground cumin
1 tsp ground coriander
¼ tsp ground ginger
1kg butternut squash, peeled, deseeded and cut into chunks
1.5 litre vegetable stock
salt and freshly ground black pepper
a little finely grated lemon zest
1 tbsp Greek yoghurt

To serve
150g mozzarella cherries (mini balls of mozzarella), or a ball of mozzarella, torn into pieces
2 tbsp coriander leaves
a pinch of ground cumin
a drizzle of chilli oil

Heat the olive oil in a large pan and fry the onion until soft, about 2 minutes, before adding the spices. Cook for a minute or until they become fragrant. Throw in the diced squash and stir well, coating it in the spices. Cook gently for 5 minutes.

Pour in the stock and bring to the boil, then reduce the heat, cover and simmer gently for 20 minutes or until the squash is tender. Cool for a minute or so, then blend until smooth in a food processor. Season to taste with salt and pepper, and stir in the lemon zest and yoghurt. (You could freeze the soup now.)

Pour into warm bowls and drop a few mini mozzarella balls or pieces into the centre of each – they will start to ooze. Scatter with coriander leaves and ground cumin before finishing with a drizzle of chilli oil. (Or you could try croûtons or truffle oil instead of the coriander and chilli oil.)

Cheese and Chive Savoury Scones

These are particularly delicious with the Curried Squash Soup on page 25 but are great with any other soup in this chapter.

MAKES 10–12

450g self-raising flour
150g salted butter, cubed
½ tsp bicarbonate of soda
2 eggs
5 tbsp milk, plus a little extra for brushing
½ tsp English mustard powder
1 tbsp chopped chives
30g Cheddar cheese, grated, plus a little extra to garnish
60g Feta cheese, crumbled

Preheat the oven to 200°C/Gas mark 6. Have ready a non-stick baking tray.

Blitz the flour, butter and bicarbonate of soda in a food processor until like breadcrumbs. Place in a large bowl.

Mix together the eggs, milk, mustard powder and chives and add to the flour. Add the cheeses, then mix to combine to a soft dough. Add a little more milk if needed.

Roll the dough out on a lightly floured surface to 2.5cm thickness, then cut roughly into ten to twelve triangles.

Place these triangles on the lined baking tray and brush the tops with milk. Bake in the preheated oven for 15 minutes or until golden brown. Remove from the oven, sprinkle with some cheese and leave to cool slightly, if you can wait! They are good hot or cold and they freeze well: once cold place them in a freezer bag so they won't stick together.

Savoyard Vegetable Soup with Petit Tomme

I had this soup and cheese 'combo' on the slopes in Chamonix and loved it. It's a perfect ski food and as an ex-chalet girl – right up my street. You can substitute the tomme and French bread for 'ciabatta dumplings' for a bigger dinner soup!

SERVES 4

50g butter
4 carrots, diced
3 leeks, finely sliced
4 parsnips, diced
2 large potatoes, diced
salt and freshly ground black pepper
a glug of brandy
1.5 litres vegetable stock
300ml full-fat milk

To serve
8 slices French bread
150g Petit Tomme cheese or
    Gruyère cheese, rind discarded,
    thinly sliced
1 tbsp chopped parsley

Heat the butter in a large pan and add the vegetables along with a pinch of salt. Cover with a lid and reduce the heat. Allow the vegetables to soften for 10 minutes, stirring frequently.

Add a glug of brandy and the stock, cover and simmer gently for 10 minutes or until the vegetables are tender.

Now add the milk to the pan and warm through but do not boil as the soup will curdle. (If it does you can simply purée the soup.) Check the seasoning.

Meanwhile lightly toast the French bread slices. Keep the grill on. Place a slice of cheese on top of each piece of French bread.

Serve the soup in heatproof bowls then top each bowl with a piece of cheesy bread. Place the bowls of soup on a baking tray and pop them under the grill for a minute to melt the cheese. Scatter with chopped parsley and serve.

Ciabatta Dumplings

These little dumplings are perfect to serve with all kinds of home-made soups. They use up any stale bread you have lying about, although I like them best when I have leftover ciabatta. Make up a double batch and pop them in the freezer ready to bulk up any soup.

MAKES 16–18

200g stale ciabatta bread, cut into
  1cm cubes
200ml milk
salt
1 tsp finely ground black pepper
1 tbsp of chopped herbs such as
  parsley, dill, tarragon, thyme
40g Parmesan cheese, finely grated
1 egg, lightly beaten
1 tbsp plain flour
2 tbsp olive oil

Place the ciabatta in a bowl. Warm the milk with a pinch of salt and the black pepper then pour over the bread. Leave it for 10 minutes.

Stir in the herbs, Parmesan, egg and flour. Stir well to form a sticky dough that holds its shape.

With slightly wet hands shape the mixture into walnut-sized balls then fry in a little olive oil for 5 minutes until golden brown all over and cooked through.

Serve on top of any soup.

Monique's French Onion Soup

Many school holidays were spent with my Parisian godmother Monique. She was truly French and good food, even smelly cheeses, were central to life, as was wine. This soup is a classic, one she made for me often. Serve with a bowl of green beans or asparagus on the side if you like.

SERVES 4

30g butter
300g onions, thinly sliced
1 tsp brown sugar
2 tsp plain flour
200ml white wine
1.5 litres good-quality beef stock or
  dark chicken stock
salt and freshly ground black pepper
a little squeeze of lemon juice

To serve
8 slices of stale baguette
100g Gruyère cheese, finely grated
sprinkling of parsley (optional)

Preheat the oven to 180°C/Gas mark 4.

Heat the butter in a large pan and cook the onion and sugar over a medium heat for 15 minutes until the onion is caramelised and golden brown in colour.

Now stir in the flour and cook for 2 minutes. Pour in the wine, stirring all the time, then add the stock. Simmer gently for 15 minutes, then season to taste, adding a little lemon juice as well. (At this point, you can cool the soup and freeze if desired.)

Meanwhile bake the sliced baguette for 8–10 minutes until crisp. Pile each one high with grated cheese and place back in the oven for 2 minutes to start the cheese melting.

Serve the soup in bowls, then top with a couple of your cheesy croûtons and sprinkle with parsley if you wish.

Comforting Pea and Ham Soup with a Hint of Mint

Yes, I use canned peas in this and why not? The soup is quick, easy and delicious and my family love it!

SERVES 4

1 tbsp olive oil
1 onion, finely chopped
1.5 litres chicken, ham or vegetable stock
1 x 600g bag frozen peas
200g canned, drained peas
12 or so mint leaves (or 1 tsp mint sauce)
salt and freshly ground black pepper

To serve
4 slices of chunky ham, diced
4 tbsp crème fraîche
a few mint leaves, torn
olive oil

Heat the olive oil in a large pan and fry the onion until soft, about 2 minutes. Pour in the stock, bring to the boil and add all the peas. Bring back to the boil, then cook for 3 minutes. Stir in the mint leaves.

Blend the soup until smooth, adjusting the consistency with more stock if needed. Season well.

Add a little diced ham to the bottom of each serving bowl, then pour over the hot soup. Top with a dollop of crème fraîche, a little more diced ham, and a few torn mint leaves. Drizzle over some olive oil, give a final grind of black pepper and serve.

Auntie Sylvia's Jewish Chicken Soup

My Auntie Sylvia cooks this all the time. It's medicine for the soul or 'Jewish penicillin' as it is popularly known and a dish that every Jewish woman knows how to cook from birth. It is perfect on a winter's evening or when you are feeling a little under the weather. Who needs to go to the pharmacy when you can have this…

SERVES 4

1 leftover roast chicken carcass, with any meat picked from the bones
2 onions, chopped
3 celery stalks, chopped
2 garlic cloves, chopped
3 bay leaves
a few black peppercorns
2 handfuls of Jewish fine egg noodles, or spaghetti broken into small pieces
salt and freshly ground black pepper
1 tbsp chopped parsley
1 tbsp chopped dill

For the matzo dumplings
3 eggs
130g matzo meal, or matzo crackers blitzed to crumbs

Place the chicken carcass, the veg and flavourings in a saucepan, cover with cold water and bring to the boil. Simmer for 30 minutes (every now and then skim off any of the foam that gathers on the surface).

For the dumplings beat the eggs in a bowl with 4 tbsp water. Season with some salt and pepper, then gradually stir in the matzo meal. Wet your hands then roll the paste into 16 small balls. They will expand as they cook, so don't go too large. Keep to one side.

After 30 minutes strain the chicken reserving the stock. Pick out some of the cooked veg and reserve. Place the stock on the heat and add the matzo balls. Cover and gently simmer for 10 minutes, then stir in the noodles. Cook for a further 10 minutes before stirring through some of the cooked veg and any picked pieces of chicken, allowing them to warm though.

Check the seasoning once more then serve in large comforting bowls, sprinkled with the chopped herbs.

Mummy's Minestrone Soup

My mother has made this soup ever since I was little and it's everything a soup should be – comforting, filling and delicious. This is purely a guideline of a recipe: there is no right or wrong with it. If you don't have any green beans don't panic! If you have a load of leeks throw them in and if you have leftover pasta from last night you can add that to the recipe as well. It's a one-pot wonder of a dish.

SERVES 4

2 tbsp olive oil
1 large onion, finely chopped
150g bacon lardons or chunky ham pieces
2 large carrots, finely chopped
3 celery stalks, finely chopped
2 garlic cloves, crushed
1 red chilli, finely chopped
2 x 400g cans chopped tomatoes
about 400ml vegetable or chicken stock
150g spaghetti, broken into small pieces
100g green beans, cut into 2cm pieces
1 large handful kale, chopped, or baby spinach leaves
2 tbsp fresh oregano or chopped parsley leaves
salt and freshly ground black pepper
Parmesan shavings, to serve

Heat the oil in a large pan and fry the onion, lardons, carrot and celery until starting to soften, about 2 minutes. Add the garlic and chilli and cook for 30 seconds before stirring in the tomatoes and stock. Bring to a simmer then add the pasta if you are using raw.

Simmer gently for 5 minutes, stirring occasionally, then stir in the green beans, kale and herbs. (If you are using leftover pasta that is already cooked now is the time to add it.) Cook for a further 3 minutes until the beans are tender but with a slight crunch to them. Check seasoning.

Serve in warm bowls with a few shavings of Parmesan and a little more black pepper.

Smoky Bean and Haddock Soup with Garlic Mayo Toasts

I love smoked haddock. It is so full of flavour you don't have to make much effort for a dish that tastes great, leaving you more time to curl up on the sofa. This rich and creamy winter soup is also ready in no time.

SERVES 4

2 tbsp olive oil
25g butter
2 leeks, finely sliced
2 celery stalks, finely chopped
1 fennel bulb, finely chopped
1 garlic clove, crushed
500g potatoes, cut into 1cm cubes
500ml fish or vegetable stock
500ml milk
a good pinch of saffron strands
1 x 400g can cannellini beans,
   drained and rinsed
200g raw prawns, peeled
600g smoked haddock, undyed or
   naturally dyed, skinned and cut
   into 2cm pieces
1 tbsp roughly chopped dill
salt and freshly ground black pepper

For the garlic mayo toasts
8 long thin slices of French bread
6 tbsp good-quality mayonnaise
1 large garlic clove, crushed

Preheat the oven to 180°C/Gas mark 4. Bake the French bread slices for 5 minutes until golden brown and crisp. Set to one side.

Mix together the mayonnaise and garlic. Season well with salt and pepper.

Heat the olive oil and butter in a large pan and add the leeks, celery, fennel, garlic and potatoes. Cover with a piece of baking paper and cook gently for 10 minutes.

Pour in the stock and milk. Add a pinch of saffron and bring to the boil. Simmer gently until the vegetables are soft, about another 5 minutes.

Use a stick blender to blend half the soup – you only want to blend enough to thicken it rather than making it completely smooth. (You could freeze at this stage if you wanted to before any fish is added.)

Place the soup back on the heat and add the beans, prawns and haddock. Simmer gently until the prawns are pink and cooked though, a couple of minutes only.

Check the seasoning. Pour the soup into bowls and scatter with dill. Serve with the French toasts spread with garlic mayo on the side, ready for dunking.

Chicken

Chicken is THE staple on everyone's weekly shopping list. It's so versatile and most importantly it's quick to cook when you have hungry mouths to feed after school and work. Most mid-week menus contain chicken somewhere but you don't have to just stick to chicken breast and thighs. If you spatchcock a whole chicken it will be ready in 45 minutes (see page 61). Who said you can't have a mid-week roast?

From my Lemon Chicken Schnitzel (see page 49) to Tandoori Chicken Skewers (see page 40), chicken can play host to a world of flavours. Its mild-flavoured meat can be given a huge boost with any number of herbs and spices, transforming it from average to mouth-watering in no time at all!

Quick Tandoori Chicken Skewers

This is your curry-hit-in-a-hurry and it's a perfect way of jazzing up simple chicken breasts. It smells amazing as it cooks. I make a quick mint and yoghurt sauce and instead of the usual strongly flavoured raw onion salad, I like to serve it with its milder cousin: a lightly pickled onion and carrot salad. All you really need then is a naan bread… Supper is sorted.

SERVES 4

3–4 chicken breasts, skinned
100g natural yoghurt
1 tsp ground cumin
½ tsp ground turmeric
½ tsp chilli powder
1 tsp garam masala
1 tbsp tomato purée
2 garlic cloves, grated
3cm piece of fresh root ginger, grated, or 1 tsp ready-chopped ginger

For the mint and yoghurt sauce

8cm piece of cucumber, deseeded and grated
200g natural yoghurt
2 tbsp chopped mint
salt and freshly ground black pepper

For the salad

3 tbsp caster sugar
2 tbsp white wine vinegar
1 white onion, very thinly sliced
2 carrots, cut into matchsticks
6 radishes, sliced
a pinch of chilli flakes
1 tbsp chopped parsley

You will need eight bamboo skewers soaked in water for 30 minutes or eight metal ones.

Cut the chicken into 3cm chunks. Mix together the yoghurt, cumin, turmeric, chilli powder, garam masala, tomato purée, garlic and ginger. Add the chicken chunks and coat well. Leave for 10 minutes or better still marinate overnight.

For the sauce, squeeze out any excess water from the cucumber, then place in a bowl and add the yoghurt and mint. Mix well, seasoning just before serving.

For the salad mix together the sugar and vinegar. If the sugar won't dissolve easily pop it in the microwave for 15 seconds. Add the onion, carrot and radishes. Stir well and leave to sit for 10 minutes. Once the carrot has softened drain off the liquid then stir through the chilli and parsley.

Preheat the grill and cover the grill pan with foil.

Thread the chicken on to the skewers. Pop under the grill for about 4–5 minutes on each side.

Serve the skewers with the cooling yoghurt dip, the salad and some naan bread to mop up any juices.

Chicken and Spinach Sliders with Cumin Mayo

Anybody who knows me knows that Monday and Tuesday nights are often leftover nights in our household after lots of cooking over the weekend and bits and pieces to be used up in the fridge. There is often meat leftover from the Sunday roast and it would be a shame not to use these tasty morsels for a quick and simple treat.

SERVES 2

150g leftover roast chicken, shredded
1 tsp cumin seeds
3 tbsp mayonnaise
1 tbsp olive oil
½–1 tbsp chipotle chilli paste
a dash of lime juice
salt and freshly ground black pepper
a handful of baby spinach leaves
4 small bread rolls

Preheat the grill.

Toast the cumin seeds in a dry pan for 2 minutes then grind in a pestle and mortar until fine. Mix the ground seeds into the mayonnaise and set to one side.

Heat the olive oil for a minute in a medium pan, add the chicken and fry for 2 minutes before stirring in the chipotle paste. Cook for a further minute to warm through. Remove from the heat and add a squeeze of lime juice. Season well and set to one side to cool slightly.

Cut the rolls in half, then toast under the grill, cut-side up.

Once golden spread a layer of the cumin mayonnaise on the bottom half of the roll, top with the warm chicken and spinach leaves and finally the top of the roll. Serve whilst warm and juicy.

Chicken Maryland

My mother used to make this when I was a kid. My sister and I thought it was the height of sophistication because anything American was 'cool'. Kids still love it today and I think that's down to the combination of sweet and savoury flavours. I loved it as a mid-week meal and now my son loves it too! Serve it with roast potato wedges, fried bananas and a watercress salad.

SERVES 4

4 chicken breasts, skinless
salt and freshly ground black pepper
200g fresh breadcrumbs
1 tsp cayenne pepper (or paprika)
2 eggs, beaten
a good glug of olive oil

For the accompaniments
3 large potatoes, cut into wedges
5 garlic cloves, in their skin, lightly
　crushed
½ tsp chilli flakes
3 tbsp olive oil ·
2 bananas, slightly green ones work
　best
1 tbsp olive oil
watercress salad

Preheat the oven to 200°C/Gas mark 6.

Season the chicken breasts with salt and pepper and the breadcrumbs with cayenne pepper. Dip each breast in the egg, coat in the breadcrumbs, then pop them back in the egg and breadcrumbs for a second time.

Place the potato wedges in a baking tray with the garlic, chilli flakes, seasoning and the olive oil and roast for 20 minutes.

Fry the chicken on both sides in a little olive oil until golden brown then place on the baking tray with the potatoes. Roast for a further 20 minutes or until the potatoes are tender and the chicken is golden brown and firm when gently pressed.

Peel and slice the bananas on a diagonal so that they are around 1.5cm thick. Fry the bananas on both sides in a little oil until golden brown, then season with a little black pepper.

Serve the chicken alongside the spicy potato wedges, fried bananas and a fresh watercress salad.

Chicken Cornflake Hotpot

With a teenager in the house there is always a box of cornflakes in the cupboard. However these little golden flakes don't just make an appearance at breakfast: they are perfect for adding crunch to dishes and can be used on top of shepherds' pie or even used to coat chicken breasts. If you are not a cornflake family try Rice Krispies or even a bag of plain tortilla crisps crunched up.

You can use any veggies you have in the fridge so don't panic if you don't have everything in the list below.

SERVES 4–6

8 chicken thighs, skinned and cut
   into 4 pieces each
2 tbsp olive oil
200g bacon lardons or chopped
   smoked bacon
1 onion, diced
2 carrots, chopped
2 parsnips, chopped
2 celery stalks, chopped
200g mushrooms, quartered
½ small swede, chopped
3 tbsp plain flour
125ml white wine
350ml chicken stock
1 tbsp chopped tarragon leaves

For the topping
2 large potatoes, thinly sliced into
   rounds
25g butter, melted
a large handful of cornflakes, lightly
   crushed
40g Parmesan cheese, freshly grated

Preheat the oven to 200°C/Gas mark 6.

Fry the chicken pieces in a little oil in a casserole dish until brown. Add the bacon and cook until crispy then add the diced veggies and stir well before stirring in the flour.

Cook the flour for a minute, pour in the wine stirring all the time. Add the stock and tarragon to the pan and mix well. Bring to the boil and check the seasoning.

Remove from the heat, cover the top with sliced potatoes then brush with a little butter.

Bake for 20 minutes after which sprinkle over the cornflakes and cheese then pop back in the oven for a further 10 minutes or until the potatoes are cooked, then serve.

Rosemary Chicken with Roasted Pecans, Squash and Blue Cheese

Tray-bakes are the one-pot wonder of the oven, made with little effort and maximum flavour. I love here the combinations of sweet butternut squash with its spice pairing made in heaven, cinnamon, along with tangy blue cheese, crunchy pecans and herby roast chicken.

SERVES 4

8 chicken thighs, boned, excess fat removed, skin on
400g butternut squash, peeled, deseeded and cut into big chunks
½ tsp ground cinnamon
a few sprigs of rosemary
2 tbsp olive oil
salt and freshly ground black pepper
40g pecan halves
50g blue cheese, such as Stilton or Gorgonzola

Preheat the oven to 200°C/Gas mark 6.

Place the squash in a large roasting tin. Sprinkle with cinnamon, then add the rosemary and oil. Season well.

Nestle the chicken thighs in between the chunks of squash, season the skin then roast for 20 minutes.

After 20 minutes add the pecans. Cook for a further 10 minutes, then remove the roasting tin from the oven.

Crumble the cheese over the chicken, then tuck in and enjoy.

Grandma's Lemon Chicken Schnitzel with Poached Egg and Anchovies

My mother always made this for Josh when he stayed for a sleepover: he loved the crunchy texture and the sharp flavour of the lemon with the gooey poached egg. You can easily make a few schnitzels and freeze them so that all the messy work is already done for another night.

SERVES 2

2 chicken breasts, skinless
2 tbsp plain flour
salt and freshly ground black pepper
50g stale breadcrumbs
finely grated zest of 1 lemon
3 eggs
50g unsalted butter
6 anchovies in oil (optional)
1 tbsp capers, drained
a little lemon juice
1 tbsp olive oil
a few rocket leaves, to serve

Place the chicken breasts in between two pieces of clingfilm. Use a meat mallet or rolling pin to bash them out until they are 3mm thick.

Put the flour in a bowl and season with salt and pepper. In another bowl mix together the breadcrumbs and lemon zest. In a third bowl beat one of the eggs.

Dip the chicken escalopes in seasoned flour, then beaten egg and finally breadcrumbs.

Melt the butter in a small pan then add the anchovies. Use a wooden spoon to help break them up. Stir in the capers, a little lemon juice and a good amount of black pepper.

Heat some water in a saucepan, bring to the boil, turn down to a simmer and crack the two remaining eggs in. Turn off the heat and let the eggs poach slowly while you fry the chicken.

Heat the oil in a frying pan and fry the chicken on each side for 2–3 minutes until golden brown.

Once cooked through, remove from the pan and drain off any excess oil on some kitchen paper. Keep the chicken warm if the eggs are not ready.

Serve each chicken schnitzel topped with a poached egg, scattered with rocket leaves and drizzled with the anchovy butter.

Roly-poly Chicken

This is my take on a chicken Kiev but it's slightly healthier as it's baked rather than fried. You can use this method of cooking over and over again not only with chicken but with pork and fish. Get experimenting with stuffings too. Here I've used Gruyère cheese and ham but I also love a little bit of herby cream cheese and sun-dried tomatoes or pesto and Parmesan.

SERVES 2

2 chicken breasts, skinless
salt and freshly ground black pepper
2 slices of smoked ham
40g Gruyère or Tomme or Cheddar
    cheese, coarsely grated
3 tbsp plain flour
2 eggs, beaten
75g dried breadcrumbs
1 tbsp olive oil

To finish
50g butter
6 small sage leaves
a little lemon juice

Place the chicken breasts on a clingfilm-covered board. Use a sharp knife to cut through the thickest part of the breast, but don't go all the way through, just create a flap so you can open it up like a book. Repeat with the other breast. Cover them with clingfilm then use a meat mallet or rolling pin to bash them out until about 5mm thick.

Season the escalopes then lay a slice of ham over each one, not letting it go over the edges. Place a line of grated cheese down the middle. Roll each of the chicken breasts up tightly, tucking in the edges. You can use the clingfilm to help. Use a toothpick to secure the end.

Preheat the oven to 180°C/Gas mark 4 and line a baking tray with baking paper.

Put the flour in one bowl and season with salt and pepper. Put the beaten egg in a second bowl and the breadcrumbs in a third. Coat each rolled chicken breast in the flour, then the egg, then the breadcrumbs. Pop them back into the egg and breadcrumbs making sure they are coated all over. You can freeze the chicken breasts at this point.

Place the chicken rolls on your lined baking tray and drizzle with olive oil. Roast in the preheated oven for 20 minutes or until firm.

Melt the butter in small frying pan then add the sage leaves. Fry for a minute then remove from the heat. Season and finish with a little lemon juice. Serve the cooked chicken with a little of the butter sauce for dipping!

Marmalade and Balsamic Chicken

I love marmalade whether it's slathered on crumpets or the bread Paul makes. I also like to add it to savoury dishes, as it combines sweet and savoury flavours which everyone loves. I've used chicken breasts here but if you fancy it or are out to impress you can easily use duck breasts instead – use what you have!

SERVES 4

4 chicken breasts, skin on
salt and freshly ground black pepper
1 tbsp olive oil
3 spring onions, sliced

For the marmalade sauce
4 tbsp marmalade
1 tsp Dijon mustard
1 garlic clove, grated
juice of 1 small orange
1 tbsp balsamic vinegar
1 tbsp thyme leaves
150ml chicken stock

Season the skin of the chicken then place skin-side down in a large frying pan with a little oil. Leave to fry over a high heat for 5 minutes or until you have really crispy skin. Drain off any excess fat.

Meanwhile for the sauce mix together the marmalade, mustard, garlic, orange juice, balsamic vinegar and thyme leaves. Season well.

Turn the chicken over, then pour in the sauce. Reduce the heat, pour in the stock and cover with a lid. Cook on the hob for 15 minutes, stirring occasionally. If the sauce becomes too thick, add a little more stock.

Once cooked serve the chicken and its sticky sauce with a scattering of spring onions. Serve with rice or new potatoes.

Chipotle Chilli Chicken Bake with Avocado and Lime Salad

We love chilli in the Hollywood household! We put chilli in anything and everything whether it's fresh, dried, chilli sauce or chilli paste. If you are not a fan or if you have little ones to feed you can simply reduce the amount. However if you are like me you can always add a bit more! And here I have also given you a cooling salad which is all that is needed…

SERVES 4

4 chicken legs, skin on, bone in
2 tbsp clear honey
grated zest and juice of 1 lime
1 heaped tbsp chipotle chilli paste
1 tbsp olive oil
salt and freshly ground black pepper
2 red peppers, deseeded and cut into 2cm chunks
2 garlic cloves, crushed
2 red onions, roughly chopped
2 sweet potatoes, cut into 2.5cm cubes
2 tbsp coriander leaves, to serve

For the avocado and lime salad

2 ripe avocadoes, roughly chopped
4 spring onions, roughly chopped
4 large tomatoes, roughly chopped
1 tbsp toasted pine nuts
juice of 1 lime
1 tbsp olive oil

Preheat the oven to 180°C/Gas mark 4.

Make three to four cuts through the skin and down to the bone on each chicken leg.

In a wide bowl mix together the honey, lime zest and juice, chipotle paste and olive oil with a pinch of salt. Add the chicken legs along with the red peppers, garlic, onions and sweet potato.

Mix well, then tip out into a baking dish making sure the chicken is skin-side up. Roast in the preheated oven for 40 minutes or until the chicken is cooked through.

Mix all the salad ingredients together. Leave to stand but not in the fridge, until ready to serve. Season with salt and pepper.

Remove the chicken from the oven and scatter with fresh coriander. Serve alongside the avocado salad.

Mozzarella-grilled Chicken Breast with Anchovy Gremolata

Sauces are often the very thing that can make a dish but also the thing that can take the most time. This quick and easy gremolata is a great substitute for a tomato sauce, and takes minutes to prepare. I have also given you some mini roasties to complete the meal.

SERVES 2

2 chicken breasts, skinless
salt and freshly ground black pepper
1 tbsp olive oil
1 ball of mozzarella, drained and
    sliced

For the mini roasties
350g new potatoes
2 tbsp olive oil
a few sprigs of rosemary
a few strips of lemon zest
150g cherry tomatoes on the vine
    cut into small bunches
2 tbsp balsamic vinegar

For the gremolata
a large handful of parsley leaves
1 small garlic clove
grated zest of 1 lemon
3 anchovy fillets in oil, drained
1 small shallot, roughly chopped
about 4 tbsp olive oil

Preheat the oven to 220°C/Gas mark 7.

For the mini roasties boil the new potatoes for 5 minutes until par-cooked, then drain. Now place the potatoes in a roasting tin and drizzle with olive oil and some salt and pepper. Roast for 15 minutes, then remove from the oven. Add the rosemary, lemon zest and cherry tomatoes and drizzle over the balsamic vinegar. Place back in the oven for 10 minutes. Keep warm.

Preheat the grill and line a baking tray with foil.

For the gremolata blitz together the parsley, garlic, lemon zest, anchovy fillets and shallot. Once coarsely chopped drizzle in enough olive oil to make a saucy consistency. Season well.

Use a sharp knife to butterfly open the chicken breasts. To do this cut through the thickest part with a sharp knife horizontally, taking care not to go all the way through then open it up like a book. Season well then drizzle with olive oil. Pop the escalopes under the grill for 3 minutes on each side or until golden brown.

Once the chicken is cooked top with slices of mozzarella and place under the grill once more. Allow the cheese to melt and turn lightly golden brown.

Serve the chicken with a good spoonful of the gremolata and your mini roasties.

Brown Sugar 'n' Spice Mix Chicken with Tangy Coleslaw

There is a definite 'deep south' flavour to this recipe that kids love! Serve it with corn on the cob and buttery baked potato skins to keep hunger at bay…

SERVES 4

8 chicken thighs, skin on, bone in
2 tbsp Brown Sugar 'n' Spice Mix
   (see page 16)
2 tbsp olive oil

For the tangy coleslaw
1 tbsp wholegrain mustard
juice of 1 lemon
2 heaped tbsp mayonnaise
2 carrots, grated
¼ small red cabbage, finely
   shredded
¼ small white cabbage, finely
   shredded
1 tbsp chopped parsley
salt and freshly ground black pepper

Marinate the chicken in the spice mix and oil for 10 minutes.

Preheat the oven to 170°C/Gas mark 3.

Tip the chicken thighs out into an ovenproof dish making sure they are skin-side up. Cover with foil and roast in the preheated oven for 40 minutes, removing the foil 10 minutes before the end of cooking to allow the skin to become golden brown.

Make the coleslaw by mixing together the mustard, lemon juice and mayonnaise then throw in all your other ingredients. Give it a good mix and season well with salt and pepper.

When the chicken is cooked remove from the oven and serve with your tangy coleslaw.

Cider, Chicken and Sweetcorn Casserole Pie

I'm a Kentish girl at heart and we are surrounded by apple orchards providing us with delicious local cider both for drinking and cooking. I often use it in recipes after spending many summers in Normandy where cider and Calvados are sloshed into every dish possible. This is a cross between a casserole and a pie and is perfect for a mid-week meal!

SERVES 4

1 x 500g block of puff pastry
1 egg, beaten

For the chicken filling
8 skinless, boneless chicken thighs,
    cut into 4 pieces each
1 tbsp olive oil
200g smoked bacon lardons
2 leeks, sliced
2 tbsp plain flour
200ml cider
200ml chicken stock
50ml double cream
1 heaped tbsp wholegrain mustard
200g canned sweetcorn, drained

Heat the olive oil in a large pan and fry the chicken pieces until brown. Remove the chicken from the pan and set to one side. Add the bacon to the pan and cook until crisp before stirring in the leeks. Cook until soft, about 2 minutes, then stir in the flour and cook for another 2 minutes.

Gradually add the cider, stirring all the time. Bring to a simmer before pouring in the stock and cream. Simmer for a few minutes, then add the chicken back to the pan along with the mustard and sweetcorn. Reduce until thickened, about 15-20 minutes. Remove the pan from the heat and leave to cool slightly before spooning the chicken filling into a 20 x 20cm pie dish. Leave to cool.

Preheat the oven to 200°C/Gas mark 6.

Roll the pastry out until 1cm thick. Brush the lip of the pie dish with a little beaten egg. Place the rolled sheet of pastry on top of the pie so that it completely covers the filling, press the edges down firmly, then crimp. Trim off any excess pastry. Make a little hole in the middle of the pie with a sharp knife and decorate with any pastry trimmings. Brush with beaten egg.

Bake in the preheated oven for 20 minutes or until the pastry is golden brown.

Road-kill Chicken with Garlic, Fennel and Vine Tomatoes

I'm keeping this simple. There are only a few ingredients but the joy of cooking in this way is that you can have roast chicken in about 30–40 minutes. I start mine off in a large paella pan with my heavy casserole lid to weight it down before transferring it to a roasting tray where Josh lovingly refers to it as 'road-kill chicken'.

SERVES 4

1 x 1.6kg chicken
3 tbsp olive oil
2 garlic bulbs, cut in half
  horizontally
salt and freshly ground black pepper
1 large fennel bulb, cut into 8 wedges
a few sprigs of woody herbs like
  thyme, lemon thyme, rosemary,
  bay leaves
200g cherry tomatoes on the vine,
  cut into small bunches
3 tbsp balsamic vinegar

Preheat the oven to 200°C/Gas mark 6.

There are three ways to spatchcock a chicken: with a knife, with sharp poultry scissors or – the third, final and easiest way – get the butcher to do it for you!

If you are attempting it yourself, it really is not that hard. Simply place the chicken on a board. Insert a knife or scissors into the chicken parallel to it's backbone. The blade should be to one side of the backbone. Simply cut through the bone. If using a knife you could tap the handle with a rolling pin to help you get through it. Once you are all the way through and along the backbone repeat on the other side and remove that bone completely, then open it up so that it is lying flat, skin-side up. Press down on the breast-bone to help keep it flat.

Once spatchcocked, drizzle the skin with a little of the olive oil, then rub one of the halved garlic bulbs all over. Season well.

Heat a little oil in a large ovenproof pan and brown the chicken skin-side down. You can use the lid of a casserole dish to help press it flat. Once golden brown, turn it over so that it is skin-side up. Add the halved bulbs of garlic, the fennel and herbs, then drizzle with olive oil.

Place the pan in the preheated oven for 30 minutes. Then add the tomatoes and drizzle the chicken with balsamic vinegar. Roast for a further 5–10 minutes until the chicken is cooked through. Remove from the oven and leave to rest for 5 minutes before serving with any pan juices drizzled over, and the fennel, garlic and tomatoes.

Garlic-stuffed Roast Chicken with Lemon, Thyme and Honey Glaze

Roast chicken is one of life's simplest pleasures and our whole family loves it. It's so comforting and familiar that it shouldn't just be kept for Sundays. This is such a simple recipe but the honey drizzle will add a certain something so sit back and let the glorious aroma of roast chicken fill your kitchen mid-week!

SERVES 4

1 x 1.5kg whole chicken
1 garlic bulb, cut in half
1 lemon, cut into chunks
a small bunch of fresh thyme
2 carrots, cut into chunks
2 onions, cut into wedges
2 tbsp olive oil
2 tbsp clear honey
salt and freshly ground black
   pepper

For the crème fraîche and mustard mash

1kg floury potatoes, cut into large
   chunks
3 large dollops crème fraîche
50ml milk
1 heaped tbsp wholegrain mustard
3 spring onions, sliced

Preheat the oven to 190°C/Gas mark 5.

Stuff the chicken cavity with the garlic bulb, lemon chunks and thyme. Place the carrot and onion in the base of a roasting tray. Place the chicken on top.

Mix together the olive oil and honey with a good pinch of salt and lots of pepper, then drizzle over the chicken.

Cook according to the weight of the bird: i.e. 20 minutes per 500g plus 20 minutes, so a 1.5kg chicken will take 1 hour 20 minutes. After 40 minutes turn the chicken on to its breast for 30 minutes. Then turn it back again to help keep it juicy.

For the mash, boil the potatoes until tender then drain. Mash them with the crème fraîche, milk, mustard and spring onions. Season well.

When the chicken is cooked (you can check this by inserting a skewer into the thickest part of the leg: if the juices run clear it is done), place on a board and remove the garlic from the cavity.

Remove the garlic cloves from their skins and squash them into the pan juices. Add a dash of water if necessary to create a sauce, season well and heat through quickly while you are carving the bird. Drizzle the sauce over the chicken on each plate, and serve with the crème fraîche mash and seasonal vegetables.

Fajitas with all the Trimmings

If you don't have time, shop-bought salsa and guacamole are fine but if you do, here are some easy recipes.

SERVES 4

4 skinless chicken breasts, cut into thin strips
1 large red onion, finely sliced
1 red pepper, deseeded and sliced
1 yellow pepper, deseeded and sliced
1 orange pepper, deseeded and sliced
2 tbsp Spicy Fajita Mix (see page 19)
1 tbsp olive oil

For the salsa

1 tbsp olive oil
200g cherry tomatoes, quartered
1 heaped tsp brown sugar
1 tsp vinegar, (white wine, malt or red wine)
salt and freshly ground black pepper

For the guacamole

2 large ripe avocados, peeled and stoned
2 tbsp chopped coriander
juice of 1 lime
2 spring onions, finely sliced

To serve

8 soft tortilla wraps
a handful of coriander leaves
2–3 dollops of soured cream
about 50g Cheddar cheese, grated
2 limes, cut into wedges

Place the chicken, onion and peppers in a large bowl with the fajita mix and the olive oil. Mix everything together. Leave to stand whilst you make the salsa and guacamole.

For the salsa heat the oil in a small frying pan, add the tomatoes and cook for 2 minutes until starting to soften. Stir in the brown sugar and vinegar. Cook until slightly reduced then season with salt and pepper.

For the guacamole mash together the avocados, coriander and lime juice to taste. Once roughly mashed stir in the sliced spring onions and season with salt and pepper.

Fry the marinated chicken and pepper mix in the oil until the chicken is cooked through, about 6 minutes.

Warm your tortilla wraps in the microwave or wrap in foil and pop in a medium oven for a few minutes.

Serve your spicy chicken on a platter in the middle of the table with your tortillas, fresh coriander and lime wedges alongside bowls of salsa, guacamole, grated cheese and soured cream.

Spanish Chicken Pieces with Garlic and Chorizo

My dad always cooked chicken with chorizo as he had lived in Madrid. He loved the rich earthy flavours of the sausage with garlic and paprika and now this is a staple week-day dinner.

SERVES 4

4 chicken thighs and 4 chicken
    drumsticks, bone in, skin on
salt and freshly ground black pepper
1 tbsp olive oil
1 onion, sliced
200g cooking chorizo, chopped
1 red pepper, deseeded and sliced
2 garlic cloves, finely sliced
a pinch of saffron strands (optional)
1 bay leaf
a few sprigs of thyme
125ml white wine
2 x 400g cans chopped tomatoes
150ml chicken stock
1 x 400g can chickpeas, drained and
    rinsed
2 tbsp chopped parsley

Season the chicken well. Heat the oil in a casserole dish then fry the chicken until golden brown. Remove from the pan and set to one side.

Add the onions to the casserole and cook until starting to soften, about 2 minutes, then throw in the chorizo. Once the chorizo is crisp add the red pepper, garlic, saffron, bay leaf and thyme, followed by the wine.

Stir, then simmer until the wine has reduced by half. Pour in the canned tomatoes and stock before placing the browned chicken back in the pan. Cover with a lid and simmer gently for 30 minutes or until the chicken is cooked through and tender.

Once the chicken is cooked, add the chickpeas, stir and cook for a further 5 minutes before scattering with parsley. Serve with crusty bread or boiled rice.

Mince

I think everyone's weekly shop will contain mince but usually just minced beef ready to make spaghetti Bolognese for dinner. However, the supermarkets have a variety of minced meats such as pork, turkey and lamb which are perfect for making family-friendly meals.

Meatballs and patties are easy and often I make a double batch: I will freeze half on a baking tray until solid, then pop them in a freezer bag. It means that some of the hard, messy work is already done for you.

Persian Lamb with Mint, Lime and Spinach

Middle-Eastern lamb dishes are great favourites with me. Roasted legs, braised shanks and tagines are great but mid-week they can take a while to cook to become tender. This recipe combines the heady aromas of Persian cooking with quick-cooking mince. I like to eat it with flatbreads and lots of colourful garnishes but if you don't have any bread you can always serve it with basmati rice.

SERVES 2

400g minced lamb
1 tbsp olive oil
1 tsp ground cumin
¼ tsp ground nutmeg
½ tsp ground cinnamon
1 garlic clove, crushed
1 tbsp tomato purée
50ml stock
1 tbsp maple syrup or clear honey
50g stoned prunes, halved
400g baby spinach leaves, washed
1 tbsp chopped mint leaves
salt and freshly ground black pepper
finely grated zest and juice of 1 lime

To serve

4 tbsp hummus (shop-bought or
    home-made)
2 spring onions, sliced
a few mint leaves
2 tbsp natural yoghurt
2–4 flatbreads
lime wedges

In a large pan fry the lamb in a little oil, breaking it up as it cooks. When it is brown tip it into a sieve to get rid of the excess fat.

Place the meat back in the pan and add the cumin, nutmeg, cinnamon and garlic. Fry for a couple of minutes before stirring in the tomato purée, add a dash of stock then the honey, prunes, spinach leaves and mint. Cook until the spinach has wilted. Season well then add the lime zest and juice.

Mix the hummus with a little hot water to loosen it slightly.

Spread a little hummus over the base of two shallow bowls, then serve the lamb on top (this helps to just warm the hummus through). Scatter with sliced spring onions, mint leaves and a dollop of yoghurt before serving with warm flatbreads and lime wedges.

Pork and Mushroom Crespelle

Crespelle are thin Italian pancakes just like a French crêpe. But they can be savoury as well as sweet and as such make a great alternative to pasta, rice and potatoes. You can buy ready-made savoury pancakes now but on a day when you have a little more time on your hands make them yourself. You could also make a double batch of pancakes, stack them between pieces of baking paper, wrap the stack in clingfilm and then simply pop them in the freezer for another day.

SERVES 6

For the filling
500g minced pork
50g butter
1 tbsp olive oil
1 onion, finely chopped
1 garlic clove, crushed
250g mushrooms, preferably
   chestnut, sliced
80g Parmesan cheese, freshly grated
225g ricotta cheese (cream cheese is
   a good substitute)
½ tsp ground nutmeg
1 tbsp chopped chives or tarragon
salt and freshly ground black pepper

For the pancakes (if pushed for time, buy ready-made)
150g plain flour
1 large egg
350ml milk
sunflower or vegetable oil

To finish
200g cherry tomatoes, quartered
1 x ball of mozzarella, drained and
   cubed
40g Parmesan cheese, freshly grated
a few basil leaves

For the filling, fry the pork in the butter and oil until golden then add the onion, garlic and mushrooms. Cook until the mushrooms are soft, then leave everything to cool.

Mix the Parmesan, ricotta, nutmeg and chives into the cooled pork and mushrooms. Season.

For the pancakes whisk together the flour, egg and half the milk. Then whisk in the remaining milk. You want the batter to be the consistency of double cream. Season with salt and pepper.

One at a time fry 12 pancakes. Heat a little oil in a 20cm pancake pan and when hot, add a ladleful of the batter. Swirl to cover the base of the pan. Leave until set, then turn over and cook the other side. Each should take about 2 minutes to make. Keep warm between pieces of parchment paper.

Preheat the oven to 180°C/Gas mark 4.

To assemble the dish take a pancake and add a spoonful of the pork and ricotta mixture in a line down one side. Fold in the ends and roll up to create a long parcel. Repeat with the remaining pancakes and mixture (these are now ready to freeze).

Place the pancakes in an ovenproof dish roughly 20 x 30cm, then scatter over the tomatoes and mozzarella. Sprinkle with Parmesan and some black pepper.

Bake in the preheated oven for 20 minutes or until golden brown, then scatter with basil leaves.

Fiery Pork Cottage Pie

I love cottage pie – it's warm, rich and comforting. So I've come up with a modern take on a traditional recipe using pork and lots of veg and adding just a hint of fiery spices for a bit of extra fire for when it's chilly out there!

SERVES 6

800g minced pork
olive oil
3 tsp smoked paprika
1 tsp chilli flakes, or more
1 tsp ground cinnamon
1 onion, diced
2 large carrots, diced
2 celery stalks, diced
2 garlic cloves, crushed
250g mushrooms, quartered
1 heaped tbsp plain flour
2 tbsp tomato purée
150ml red wine
500ml beef stock
2 tbsp Worcestershire sauce
200g baby spinach leaves

For the topping
1kg potatoes, quartered
salt and freshly ground black pepper
100ml milk
40g butter
100g Cheddar cheese, grated

Heat 2 tbsp of the olive oil in a large pan, then fry the mince, breaking it up with a wooden spoon, until browned. Stir in the paprika, chilli flakes and cinnamon. Cook for 2 minutes coating the meat in all the spices. Remove the meat from the pan and set to one side.

Add the veg to the fat in the pan, along with a little more oil if needed. Fry for a couple of minutes before adding the flour. Stir well, cook for 2 minutes, then add the tomato purée, wine, beef stock, Worcestershire sauce and the cooked beef. Simmer over a medium heat for 20 minutes or until the sauce has thickened and is coating the meat.

Boil the potatoes in lightly salted water until tender, then drain and roughly mash. Add a little of the milk (you can always add more) and all of the butter to loosen slightly. Season well.

Preheat the oven to 200°C/Gas mark 6.

Stir the spinach into the meat and allow it to wilt. Transfer everything to a 20 x 25cm ovenproof dish. Spoon the mashed potatoes over the meat, then sprinkle with the cheese.

Bake in the preheated oven for 10 minutes or until golden brown. Serve with lots of green veg.

Minced Beef Ziti with Three Cheeses

We all love lasagna but don't always have time to make it properly from scratch. Well, this dish is the answer. It tastes just like lasagna but there is no white sauce to make. Just a simple meat sauce, a bit of cooked pasta and a hot oven. Job done, dinner on the table.

SERVES 6–8

500g minced beef
2 tbsp olive oil
1 onion, diced
2 garlic cloves, crushed
2 tbsp tomato purée
150ml red wine
1 x 400g can chopped tomatoes
1 beef stock cube, dissolved in 100ml boiling water
1 tbsp tomato ketchup
1 tbsp dried oregano
a handful of basil leaves (if you have them)
salt and freshly ground black pepper
500g ziti, penne or any other pasta tubes
250g ricotta cheese
2 balls of mozzarella
80g Parmesan cheese, freshly grated

Heat the oil in a large pan and fry the onion until soft, about 2 minutes. Crumble in the minced beef breaking it up in the pan with a wooden spoon. Allow it to brown before stirring in the garlic and tomato purée.

Add in the red wine and simmer for 2 minutes, then pour in the chopped tomatoes, stock, tomato ketchup, oregano and basil. Simmer until thickened, about 20 minutes. Season well.

Preheat the oven to 180°C/Gas mark 4.

Cook the pasta in boiling water for 2 minutes less than stated on the packet, then drain.

Take a large lasagna dish and spread half of the meat mixture over the base. Then layer over that half of the cooked pasta. Now, using half of the ricotta, spoon it over the pasta in dollops, then rip one of the mozzarella balls into small pieces and scatter over as well. Season well. Repeat these layers once more, then finish with the Parmesan sprinkled over the top.

Bake in the preheated oven for 10 minutes or until golden brown and hot through, then serve with a crunchy green salad and a glass of red wine.

Chinese Spiced Beef and Noodle Stir-fry

You can make this recipe even more quickly by buying a packet of stir-fry veg instead. It just saves a little bit of time and in the Hollywood household it isn't considered cheating, it's using time efficiently.

SERVES 4–6

500g minced beef (not too lean)
2 shallots, finely chopped
2 garlic cloves, finely chopped
3 tbsp sesame (or vegetable) oil
1 red chilli, deseeded and chopped
  (optional)
2 tsp Chinese five-spice powder
1 tbsp Thai fish sauce
2 tbsp light soy sauce
200g dried egg noodles
2 carrots, cut into thin matchsticks
1 red pepper, deseeded and thinly
  sliced
2 yellow peppers, deseeded and
  thinly sliced
100g mangetout, cut in half
a handful of bamboo shoots
3 tbsp oyster sauce (optional)

To garnish
1 red chilli, deseeded and cut into
  rings
2 spring onions, sliced
2 tbsp chopped coriander leaves
4 lime wedges

In a large frying pan fry the shallot and garlic in 2 tbsp of the sesame oil until soft. Add the chilli, beef mince and five-spice powder and continue to fry until all the meat is lightly coloured. Stir in the fish sauce and soy sauce until warmed through.

Cook the egg noodles according to the packet instructions, then drain.

Stir-fry the veg in the remaining oil until cooked but still crunchy, then add to the beef along with the oyster sauce, if using, and cooked noodles. Toss everything together until hot through then serve with a scattering of fresh chilli, spring onions, coriander and a wedge of lime.

Pork Burritos with Kidney Beans and Cheese

Fajitas versus burritos versus enchiladas! This recipe can be any of those things depending on how far you take the recipe. Fajitas are self-rolled at the table, burritos must have beans in them and are ready-rolled before serving and enchiladas are baked burritos covered in sauce. Confused? Well, I am slightly, but either way you'll love this recipe and what a way to jazz up your mid-week supper!

SERVES 2–3

500g minced pork
2 tbsp olive oil
1 tsp dried oregano
1 tsp smoked paprika
1 tsp onion powder
½ tsp ground cumin
1 green chilli, finely chopped
1 x 290g jar roasted red peppers, drained
1 garlic clove
1 x 400g can kidney beans in water, drained and rinsed
2 tbsp sweet chilli sauce

To serve
6 soft tortilla wraps
about 50g Cheddar cheese, grated

In a large pan fry the pork in the oil, breaking it up, until brown. Add the oregano, paprika, onion powder, cumin and green chilli, and fry for 2 more minutes until the mix becomes fragrant.

Meanwhile blend all the roasted red peppers and the garlic together until smooth. You may need to add a little water to do this.

Pour the puréed red peppers into the mince and stir well before tipping in the kidney beans and the sweet chilli sauce. Simmer for 10–15 minutes until thick and the beans have softened slightly.

Place a tortilla wrap on a flat surface, then spoon a line of the mince mixture down the middle. Sprinkle with cheese.

Fold the ends of the wrap over the ends of the line of mince then roll it up to create an enclosed long parcel. Serve immediately.

Stuffed Marrow with Spicy Minced Lamb and Feta Crumble

Stuffed marrow is a thing of beauty and very underrated. This was a dish my mother would cook to perfection because my dad grew marrows by the ton! It's very easy, very healthy and I think crumble is to die for…

SERVES 4

1 marrow – nothing too ridiculously big
1 tbsp olive oil
1 tsp chilli flakes
salt

For the filling
500g minced lamb
100g cooking chorizo, diced
1 tbsp olive oil
1 onion, diced
1 red pepper, deseeded and diced
1 tsp smoked paprika
½ tsp cayenne pepper
a few sprigs of rosemary
1 x 400g can chopped tomatoes

For the crumble topping
40g butter
1 tbsp thyme leaves
3 tbsp pine nuts
75g fresh breadcrumbs
150g Feta cheese

Preheat the oven to 190°C/Gas mark 5.

Fry the chorizo in a little oil until crisp, then stir in the diced onion and pepper. Cook for 2 minutes on a high heat until starting to soften.

Crumble the lamb into the pan and fry until brown, then stir in the spices and rosemary. Cook for a couple of minutes then add the tomatoes. Stir well and simmer gently for 10 minutes.

Cut the marrow in half lengthways then scoop out the seeds with a spoon. Place both halves in a roasting tray.

Spoon the meat into the centre of the marrow halves, lightly cover with foil, then bake in the preheated oven for 20–25 minutes.

For the crumble topping, melt the butter in a small pan, turn the heat off, then stir in the thyme leaves, pine nuts and breadcrumbs. Leave to cool before crumbling in the Feta.

Once the marrow is tender remove the foil, sprinkle the crumble topping over the top and pop the tray and marrow back in the oven for 8–10 minutes or until the crumble is golden brown.

Uncle James's Bruschetta Burgers

My brother-in-law James makes these legendary burgers every summer, usually for a garden supper after a long hot day on the beach. Here in Kent where the beach and countryside meet, these are fast-food delicious and make me think of hot sunny Margate days. Very retro – and perfect for a quick mid-week dinner.

SERVES 4

For the patties
800g 20% fat minced beef
1 onion, finely chopped
25g butter
a handful of fresh breadcrumbs
1 tsp Dijon mustard
1 egg yolk
salt and freshly ground black pepper
1 tbsp olive oil

For the burger sauce
3 tbsp mayonnaise
1 tbsp tomato ketchup
a dash of Tabasco sauce (or soy sauce)

To serve
8 slices of Gruyère cheese
8 rashers of smoked streaky bacon
1 fresh ciabatta loaf, halved lengthways
4 pineapple rings
1 avocado, sliced
baby gem lettuce leaves

Make the burger sauce by mixing together the ingredients then seasoning with salt and pepper.

For the patties fry the onion in the butter until soft – about 2 minutes – then cool.

Mix together the mince, breadcrumbs, mustard, egg yolk and cooled onion. Season well. Divide the mix into four then shape into patties (you can freeze these now if you make a double batch).

Fry the patties in a little oil until golden brown on one side, then carefully flip them over, top with cheese and cook for 3–4 minutes depending on how you like them. If you put a lid on the pan this will help the melting (or you can put the patties under a preheated grill).

Fry the bacon until crisp, and toast the insides of the ciabatta. Cut the ciabatta halves in half.

To assemble spread a little of the burger sauce on the four pieces of toasted bread, then add a few lettuce leaves. Top with your cheesy burger then place a pineapple ring and some avocado on top. Finally break the bacon up into large pieces and scatter over. Serve with more burger sauce if you fancy it.

Lamb and Cinnamon Toastie with Quick Tomato Relish

This may sound odd but it just works. We are all used to a traditional cheese and ham toastie but this takes toasties to a new level. (Hence why at the back of the book there is a whole host of toastie ideas inspired by the success of this one.) If you don't already have one, now is the time to go and buy a toastie machine.

MAKES 4

8 slices of bread
a little butter

For the filling
500g lean minced lamb
2 tbsp olive oil
1 onion, finely chopped
1 tsp ground cinnamon
¼ tsp turmeric
1 tsp ground cumin
1 tsp ground coriander
2 garlic cloves, finely chopped
1 x 400g can chopped tomatoes
salt and freshly ground black pepper
1 tbsp chopped coriander leaves

For the quick tomato relish
1 tbsp olive oil
1 tsp mustard seeds
1 tsp garam masala
2 cardamom pods, split open
1 red chilli, finely chopped
200g cherry tomatoes, halved
1 tbsp caster sugar
1 tbsp red wine vinegar

For the filling heat the oil in a large pan and fry the onion for 2 minutes until soft, then add the spices and cook for a further minute. Crumble in the minced lamb, breaking it up with a wooden spoon and add the garlic. Cook for a few minutes until brown.

Pour in the tomatoes and cook for 10 minutes until reduced and thick – you don't want it to be watery. Season well, stir in the coriander and leave to cool.

For the relish, heat the oil in a small pan and fry the mustard seeds, garam masala and cardamom pods. Once the mustard seeds start popping throw in the chilli and cherry tomatoes. Cook for 2 minutes allowing the tomatoes to soften before stirring in the sugar and vinegar. Simmer until reduced.

When you are ready to serve and the mince is cool butter the bread then turn the buttered side out. Divide the lamb between four slices of the bread (on the non-buttered side) then place the other slices on top. You want an inside-out buttered sandwich.

Preheat the toastie machine, then cook the sandwiches until golden brown and crisp on the outside.

Serve with the warm tomato relish and a green salad.

Swedish Meatballs

Swedish meatballs are a delicious mixture of minced pork for sweetness and minced beef for meaty flavour. The pork and breadcrumbs also help to lighten the mix so that the meatballs are not too dense and heavy. In Sweden they are often accompanied by a sweet jam made from lingonberries but it's not easy to get hold of elsewhere so cranberry jelly is a perfect replacement.

SERVES 6

400g minced pork
400g minced beef
1 large egg, beaten
75g fresh breadcrumbs, soaked in
    50ml milk
1 tbsp capers, drained and chopped
    (optional)
1 tsp ground allspice
1 tbsp chopped dill
finely grated zest of 1 lemon
salt and lots of freshly ground black
    pepper
2 tbsp olive oil

For the sauce
25g butter
1 tbsp plain flour
300ml good-quality beef stock
2 tbsp crème fraîche
2 heaped tbsp cranberry jelly

To serve
2 tbsp roughly chopped dill
4 tbsp cranberry jelly (lingonberry if
    you can get it)

Mix together the pork, beef, egg, soaked breadcrumbs, capers, allspice, dill and lemon zest and season well with salt and pepper. Roll the mixture into walnut-sized balls (if you double up your mix you can now freeze these).

Fry the meatballs in a little oil for 5 minutes turning frequently until golden brown all over. Remove from the pan and set to one side.

Add a little knob of butter to the pan along with the flour. Cook the flour for a minute, scraping any caramelised bits from around the pan. Slowly stir in the stock then bring to a simmer. Stir in the crème fraîche and cranberry jelly.

Reduce the heat then place the meatballs back into the sauce and cook gently until the sauce is coating them.

Serve the meatballs and their sauce (on mashed potato, rice or traditional noodles), with a scattering of dill and a dollop of the cranberry jelly.

Keftedes (Cypriot Meatballs)

Paul and I met in Cyprus so the island has a very special place in our hearts, as does the food! This is one of those easy village recipes, hearty meatballs made with lamb and beef, flavoured with mint and cinnamon, which give them a warm, delicious Middle-Eastern fragrance. I love them especially because they freeze well – great if you suddenly have unexpected mouths to feed. The meat is bulked up with the other ingredients but the meatballs are still mouth-wateringly good to eat.

SERVES 6–8

400g minced lamb
400g minced beef
6 large potatoes
juice of 2 lemons
2 eggs, beaten
2 tbsp finely chopped parsley
1 tbsp dried mint
1 tsp ground cinnamon
½ tsp garlic powder
1 tsp mixed spice
50g fresh breadcrumbs
salt and freshly ground black pepper
olive oil, for frying

To serve
2 lemons, quartered
150g natural yoghurt

Put the minced meats into a large bowl.

Peel the potatoes and grate on the finest grater hole. Place the grated potato in a clean tea-towel and squeeze out any excess moisture.

Sprinkle the potato with the lemon juice, then add to the minced meat in the bowl along with the eggs, parsley, mint, cinnamon, garlic powder and mixed spice. Mix everything together.

Add a large handful of breadcrumbs and mix well. You only want to add enough breadcrumbs so that any moisture in the mixture is absorbed. Season well with salt and pepper.

Roll the mixture into balls about the size of a ping-pong ball (double up and freeze these if you like).

Shallow-fry the balls in batches until golden brown. Each batch will take roughly 6 minutes to cook through.

Once cooked drain on kitchen paper and serve with a squeeze of lemon and a dollop of natural yoghurt.

Thai-spiced Turkey Meatballs with Noodles and Coconut Broth

Minced turkey is available all year round but if you can't get hold of it just use minced chicken or pork. It is really low in fat but can also be low in flavour so it is perfect for the big bold flavours that characterise Thai food.

SERVES 4

500g turkey mince
50g fresh breadcrumbs
1 egg, beaten
1 garlic clove, crushed
a dash of Thai fish sauce
1 tbsp chopped coriander leaves
2 tbsp vegetable oil
2 heads of pak-choi, quartered
a handful of mangetout or sugar-snap peas (beansprouts, green beans, peas etc)

For the sauce
2 shallots or 1 onion, finely chopped
2 garlic cloves, grated
5cm piece of fresh root ginger, grated, or 1 tbsp ready-chopped ginger
1 red chilli, finely chopped
1 tsp ground cumin
2 tbsp vegetable oil
1 x 400ml can coconut milk
100ml chicken or vegetable stock
2 lemongrass stalks, crushed
a splash of Thai fish sauce
1 tsp brown sugar
lime juice

To serve and garnish
100g dried thin rice noodles
a handful of coriander leaves
4 spring onions, chopped
1 red chilli, deseeded and sliced

Mix together the turkey, breadcrumbs, egg, garlic, fish sauce and coriander. Roll into balls about the size of walnuts. Fry the meatballs in a little oil until golden brown on all sides, then remove from the pan and keep to one side.

For the sauce fry the shallot or onion, the garlic, ginger, chilli and cumin in the vegetable oil for a minute before pouring in the coconut milk and stock. Add the whole lemongrass stalks and simmer gently for 10 minutes. Fish out the lemongrass stalks and discard.

Place the meatballs into the sauce. Simmer until the meatballs are cooked through – about 6–8 minutes – then add the pak-choi and mangetout (or other veg) and cook for a further 2 minutes. Season the sauce with fish sauce, brown sugar and lime juice.

Cook and drain the noodles according to packet instructions.

Divide the noodles between four bowls, then spoon over the meatballs and soupy sauce. Garnish with coriander, spring onion and chopped chilli if you like it hot.

Sausages and All Things Porky

Both my husband and son love pork: sausages and chops. Living in Cyprus we ate a lot of pork souvla too, grilled pork pieces fragrant with oregano and wine and cooked under the vines, so I've added recipes from my travels in this dinner chapter. Pork is so versatile, delicious with rich sticky sauces, grilled or cooked my favourite way with fruit. So if you're looking to jazz up a lone pork chop or a pack of sausages, this is the chapter for you!

Cypriot Pork Kebabs with Onions and Lemon

This is a classic Cypriot dish made all over the island and a firm family favourite. Our friend Doros – who was Paul's best man at our wedding – has a little taverna in Kouklia and these are a 'nod' to his recipe – memories of balmy summer evenings sitting on the cobbled street and eating his delicious smoky souvlakia.

SERVES 4

500g pork shoulder, cut into 2.5cm
   dice
2 small red onions, or 1 large, cut
   into 2.5cm dice
3 tbsp olive oil
1 tbsp red wine vinegar
1 tbsp dried mint
1 tsp dried thyme
1 tsp ground cumin
finely grated zest of 1 lemon
salt and freshly ground black pepper

For the lemon, cumin and cucumber yoghurt
$\frac{1}{2}$ tsp cumin seeds
8 tbsp thick Greek yoghurt
10cm piece of cucumber, deseeded
   and finely chopped
juice of $\frac{1}{2}$ lemon

To serve
flatbreads or pitta
fresh mint leaves
green salad
sliced radishes

You will need eight wooden skewers soaked in water for 30 minutes or eight metal skewers.

Place the meat, onion chunks, olive oil, vinegar, mint, thyme, cumin and lemon zest in a bowl. Mix everything together. Leave to marinate for 30 minutes if you have time.

Meanwhile make the yoghurt. Toast the cumin seeds in a dry pan, then crush in a pestle and mortar. Mix together with the yoghurt, cucumber and lemon juice. Season well with salt and pepper.

Preheat a griddle pan. Thread the meat and onions on to the skewers, not packing them too tightly as this stops the meat from cooking evenly. Season well.

Cook the skewers on the griddle, turning occasionally, for 8–10 minutes.

Serve on flatbreads with the yoghurt, fresh mint and salad, sliced radishes and a squeeze of lemon juice.

Mustard and Rosemary Toad-in-the-hole with Cider Gravy

This is my twist on an all-time British favourite and it's a Twitter hit. Don't be tempted to chop the rosemary into the batter as something extraordinary happens and it will go as flat as a pancake, which makes it all a bit stodgy to say the least.

SERVES 4

8 good-quality pork sausages
2 tbsp olive oil
2 sprigs of rosemary

For the batter
125g plain flour
a good pinch of salt
3 eggs
300ml milk
1 tbsp wholegrain mustard
½ tsp English mustard powder

For the cider gravy
2 tbsp butter
2 tbsp plain flour
400ml chicken stock
100ml apple cider
a splash of apple cider vinegar
salt and freshly ground black pepper

Preheat the oven to 220°C/Gas mark 7.

Place the sausages in a baking tray. Drizzle with oil then pop in the oven for 10 minutes or until lightly golden brown.

Meanwhile for the batter whisk together the flour, salt, eggs, milk and mustards to a smooth batter.

Once the sausages are browned quickly open the oven door, throw in the rosemary sprigs and quickly pour in the batter. You want to keep the oven as hot as possible.

Bake for 20–25 minutes or until the batter is golden brown and crisp.

Whilst it's cooking make your gravy by melting together the butter and flour. Cook for 2 minutes before whisking in the chicken stock and cider. Simmer for 10 minutes then add a splash of cider vinegar and season with salt and pepper.

Serve the toad-in-the-hole with its gravy and lots of green veggies.

Ham, Ricotta and Spinach Pasta Bake

As my Twitter followers know by now I am a lover of cheese and although French cheeses are dear to my heart I'm not really fussed if they come from England, Italy or anywhere else for that matter. This is cheesy goodness in a baked pasta form.

SERVES 4

500g penne pasta
salt and freshly ground black pepper
2 tbsp olive oil
300g bacon lardons
1 x 450g bag spinach
50ml white wine
300g smoked ham, chopped
1 x 500g tub ricotta cheese
75g Parmesan cheese, grated
$\frac{1}{2}$ tsp grated nutmeg
finely grated zest of 1 lemon
150g Fontina or Brie cheese, or any
   other good strong melting cheese,
   sliced

Preheat the oven to 180°C/Gas mark 4.

Cook the pasta in salted water according to packet instructions – usually about 8 minutes – then drain, reserving some of the pasta water.

Heat the oil in a large pan, then fry the bacon lardons until becoming crisp. Add the spinach and fry until wilted. Add the white wine and simmer for 2 minutes, then tip into a bowl.

Stir the ham, ricotta, Parmesan, nutmeg and lemon zest into the spinach and season well with salt and pepper. Stir through the drained pasta with a little of the reserved cooking water to loosen everything.

Tip it into an ovenproof dish, top with slices of the Fontina cheese, then bake in the preheated oven for 15 minutes or until the top is golden brown.

Easy-peasy Spare Ribs

These are perfect to throw together then chuck in the oven before dashing off to do the afternoon school run. They take time cooking but you can fit in everything else you need to do because they're so simple to prepare and 'boy', are they good.

SERVES 4

2 racks of baby back pork ribs
300ml beef or chicken stock

For the marinade
1 tbsp English mustard
4 tbsp tomato ketchup
1 tbsp Worcestershire sauce
2 tsp Tabasco sauce
2 tbsp brown sugar
1 tbsp malt vinegar
a good pinch of chilli flakes
1 tbsp soy sauce

Mix together all the marinade ingredients in a roasting tray, then add and mix in the ribs. If you can leave them overnight to absorb the flavours, then great.

Preheat the oven to 160°C/Gas mark 3.

Add the stock to the ribs and mix, then cover the roasting tray with foil. Place in the low preheated oven and leave to cook for 2½ hours.

After this time, when the meat is tender increase the oven to 200°C/Gas mark 6. Remove the foil from the tray and cook the ribs for a further 30 minutes until the sauce is sticky. Then it's time to enjoy and get messy!

Pancetta-wrapped Pork with Asparagus

This is a really simple technique that jazzes up meat and fish and the flavours are big and punchy. Try it also with chicken breasts or even cod.

SERVES 2

2 x 200g pork escalopes
salt and freshly ground black pepper
4 sage leaves
6 slices of pancetta
1 tbsp olive oil
200g thin asparagus spears
a good splash of Marsala (optional)
40g butter
a few toasted flaked almonds

Cover the escalopes with clingfilm then use a rolling pin to bash them out until they are 5mm thick.

Season both sides with black pepper, then place a couple of sage leaves on top of each piece of pork. Wrap three slices of pancetta around each piece of pork.

Heat a large frying pan on a high heat. Add the oil and fry the pork on one side for 2 minutes then turn over and add the asparagus spears. Cook for another 2 minutes. Remove from the pan once cooked. Keep the pork and asparagus warm.

Place the pan back on the heat and add a good splash of Marsala then stir in the butter. Add the asparagus back to the pan and simmer for 1 minute. Season and then serve the pork with the asparagus and sauce and a sprinkling of toasted flaked almonds.

Hawaiian Pork Chops

Who doesn't love retro food? And this one's a classic! It used to be so exotic to mix meat and fruit, and this perfect combination with its sweet stickiness is the perfect recipe for a mid-week treat.

SERVES 4

4 x 200g pork chops
2 tsp Chinese five-spice powder
salt
2 tbsp olive oil

For the pineapple
1 x 400g can pineapple rings,
    drained but keep the juice
1 tsp tomato purée
1 tbsp brown sugar
1 tbsp dark soy sauce
1 garlic clove, thinly sliced
a little olive oil
juice of 1 lime

To serve
boiled rice
coriander leaves

Preheat the grill and cover the grill tray with foil.

Mix together the five-spice, a little salt and the oil then coat the pork chops in the mix.

Place the chops on the grill pan and grill for 4–5 minutes on each side, or until almost cooked through.

Mix together the reserved juice from the pineapple, the tomato purée, brown sugar, soy and garlic.

Heat a little olive oil in a frying pan and add the pineapple rings. Pour over the sauce. Bring to a bubble and cook for 2 minutes until slightly sticky. Add a squeeze of lime juice.

Serve the cooked chops with the pineapple rings and sauce on a bed of rice with fresh coriander.

Sausage-meat Sliders with Cranberry, Walnut and Apple Slaw

Sausage meat is a secret weapon when it comes to our quick family suppers. Once you remove the skins, the sausage meat is perfectly seasoned and ready to use without any additional chopping and mixing. It can quickly be shaped into meatballs ready for pasta sauces or stews or simply done as patties for these delicious sliders. The patties freeze well too (between sheets of greaseproof paper, then wrapped).

SERVES 2

4 sausages, skins removed
1 tbsp olive oil

For the slaw
3 tbsp crème fraîche
squeeze of lemon
1 tsp Dijon mustard
25g walnut pieces
1 sharp eating apple such as Granny Smith, cut into matchsticks
1 tbsp dried cranberries
¼ small celeriac or white cabbage, finely shredded
2 tsp chopped chives
salt and freshly ground pepper

To serve
4 slider buns, halved
watercress

Shape the sausage meat into two patties. Fry in a little olive oil until golden brown and cooked through.

Make the slaw by mixing together the crème fraîche, lemon and mustard then stirring through the nuts, apple, cranberries, celeriac and chives. Season well with salt and pepper.

Lightly toast the halved buns then top the bottom halves with the sausage patty, then some of the slaw and a little watercress. Replace the top bun and enjoy.

Stir-fried Sticky Pork with Ginger and Vegetables

Stir-fries are super-quick but don't be tempted to make it even quicker by going out and buying one of those jarred or packet sauces. You can make something so much more tasty from your cupboard ingredients or leftovers and adjust it to your taste.

SERVES 4

500g pork fillet, thinly sliced
1 tbsp toasted sesame oil
1 red onion, sliced
1 yellow pepper, deseeded and sliced
200g tenderstem broccoli, cut into
   3cm pieces
1 large carrot, sliced into thin rounds
2 heads of pak-choi, chopped, or
   ¼ small green cabbage, shredded
300g cooked egg noodles

For the sauce
1 tsp cornflour
1 tbsp water
3 tbsp soy sauce
1 tbsp dark brown sugar
2 tbsp sweet chilli sauce
5cm piece of fresh root ginger, finely
   chopped
2 garlic cloves, thinly sliced

To serve
a handful of coriander leaves
1 lime, cut into wedges
1 tbsp sesame seeds

Mix together the cornflour, water, soy, sugar, sweet chilli sauce, ginger and garlic.

Heat a wok on a high heat. Add the oil then fry the pork for 2 minutes. Remove from the wok.

Adding more oil if needed, fry the onions and peppers for a minute then add the broccoli and carrots. Stir-fry for 2–3 minutes or until the broccoli is tender but still with a good crunch to it.

Add the pak-choi, stir, then push everything to one side of the pan. Add the sauce to the empty side, cook for 30 seconds then stir everything together. Add the noodles and warm through. You can add a splash of water at this stage if the pan gets a little dry.

Serve the stir-fry in warm bowls with fresh coriander, lime wedges and a sprinkling of sesame seeds.

Sticky Moroccan Sausage with Corn Fritters

As a mum I know that there are a few ingredients most kids like but which adults secretly love just as much. Sausage and sweetcorn happily sit in both the adult- and kid-friendly camps and with a little bit of a shortcut (the quick and deliciously sticky sweet sauce) they can be transformed into a seriously tasty dinner.

SERVES 4

8 good-quality pork sausages
2 tbsp light soy sauce
2 tbsp clear honey
1 tbsp vegetable oil
1 tbsp harissa paste
5cm piece of fresh root ginger, sliced
    into 4

For the sweetcorn fritters

100g plain flour
a pinch of salt
1 tsp baking powder
2 eggs, beaten
75ml milk
1 x 325g can sweetcorn, drained
2 spring onions, chopped
1 red chilli, chopped
1–2 tbsp vegetable oil

For the garnish

1 tsp sesame seeds
1 red chilli, deseeded and sliced
2 spring onions, finely sliced

Preheat the oven to 200°C/Gas mark 6.

Place the sausages in an ovenproof dish. Mix together the soy, honey, oil, harissa and ginger and pour over the sausages. Pop the dish into the oven and roast for 25 minutes turning the sausages occasionally.

While the sausages are cooking whisk together the flour, salt, baking powder, eggs and milk to form a smooth batter. Stir in the sweetcorn, spring onions and chilli.

Heat a frying pan on a high heat and fry spoonfuls of the sweetcorn mixture in a little oil for 2 minutes on each side or until golden brown.

Serve the sausages with your sweetcorn fritters and a sprinkling of sesame seeds, chilli and spring onions.

Sausage and Winter Vegetable Bake with Mozzarella and Sage

I'm a massive fan of the lush sausages made by our local farm shop. They have loads of meat in them and very little fat. At Christmas we get loads of their little cocktail sausages and roast them in honey and mustard. This is my slightly more grown-up take on that recipe for a mid-week dinner.

SERVES 4

8 good-quality pork sausages
3 red onions, cut into wedges
3 carrots, cut into big chunks
2–3 parsnips, cut into big chunks
2 tbsp olive oil
salt and freshly ground black pepper

For the sauce and topping
1 heaped tbsp wholegrain mustard
3 tbsp clear honey
finely grated zest and juice of
    1 orange
10–12 sage leaves
1 ball of mozzarella, torn into pieces

Preheat the oven to 200°C/ Gas mark 6.

Place the onion, carrot and parsnip in an ovenproof dish large enough to hold them (plus the sausages when added). Drizzle with oil, season and toss everything together until coated.

Pop into the oven and roast for 10 minutes then add the sausages to the dish and bake for a further 10 minutes.

For the sauce mix together the mustard, honey, orange juice and zest. After 10 minutes pour the sauce over the sausages, then scatter over the sage leaves and pieces of mozzarella.

Place everything back in the oven for 10 minutes. Remove from the oven and serve with potatoes of your choice.

Beef

Beef for me falls into two very distinct categories: quick-cook or long and slow. Juicy steaks that feel a little indulgent and family-friendly mince are perfect for evenings when you need to cook an all-in-one dish to plonk on the table and sit down and eat together but the bigger joints and cheaper cuts like brisket, oxtail and stewing steak require a little bit of planning.

On weekday nights when I am on the school run these slower-cooking cuts are perfect and result in a stress-free evening on our return. I can get everything prepared in the morning or at lunchtime, pop it into a slow oven and let it work its magic.

I often cook up bigger batches of certain recipes like the Hungarian Goulash (see page 128) and Chilli Bean Bolognese (see page 115) and freeze them in individual portions ready for those days when I'm not organised and evenings when I've just run out of time or ingredients.

Flat-iron Parmesan Steak with Lamb's Lettuce

You are going to have to go to the butcher for this one but it's worth it. Flat-iron steaks are cut from the top blade so are not usually available in supermarkets. Basically, this recipe is a really simple salad but because steak is the predominant ingredient it feels more impressive than a mere salad. I've squeezed in an extra bit of cheese: I have suggested grilling some Parmesan on top of the steaks as well as serving it with Parmesan shavings. You can't get too much of a good thing and for a quick mid-week treat, it's perfect!

SERVES 2

2 x 150g flat-iron steaks (or whatever your preferred cut is)
2 tbsp olive oil
salt and freshly ground black pepper
1 tbsp Dijon mustard
a few thyme leaves
4 heaped tbsp finely grated Parmesan cheese, plus a few shavings
2 large handfuls of lamb's lettuce
2 tbsp balsamic glaze

Drizzle the steaks with 1 tbsp of the olive oil, then season well with salt and pepper.

Fry the steaks in a really hot griddle pan until nearly cooked how you like them, then remove from the pan.

Leave to rest for 4 minutes and preheat the grill.

Brush one side of each steak with a little mustard, then scatter with thyme leaves and place a big pile of Parmesan on each one. Pop the steaks under the grill for 2 minutes allowing the cheese to melt and turn golden brown.

Dress the lamb's lettuce leaves with the remaining olive oil.

Once the cheese has melted remove the steaks from the grill and slice into thin slices.

Scatter the lamb's lettuce leaves on a plate then dot with the warm steak and drizzle over the balsamic glaze, finishing with a few Parmesan shavings for a bit of extra cheesiness.

Chilli Bean Bolognese

This recipe came about when I had a small dollop of Bolognese left and I needed to bulk it up. So I scrabbled around in my larder and found a couple of cans of kidney and black-eyed beans. The recipe here is made from scratch but if you have leftovers, follow the instructions from halfway through.

SERVES 4–6

400g minced beef
2 tbsp olive oil
1 onion, very finely diced
2 celery stalks, very finely diced
½ tsp chilli flakes (optional)
2 tsp smoked paprika
100ml red wine
2 tbsp tomato purée
2 x 400g cans chopped tomatoes
100ml chicken or vegetable stock
1 x 400g can red kidney beans,
    drained and rinsed
1 x 400g can black-eyed beans
1 tbsp tomato ketchup
1 tbsp chipotle chilli sauce
salt and freshly ground black pepper

To serve
4–6 medium potatoes, baked until
    crisp
2 avocadoes, cut into 1cm chunks
a handful of coriander leaves
4 dollops of soured cream
a handful of grated cheese

Heat the olive oil in a large sauté pan. Add the onion and celery and fry for 5 minutes until soft and starting to take on colour. Add the chilli flakes and paprika.

Add the meat to the pan and fry until brown, breaking it up with a spoon.

Pour in the red wine then bring to the boil. Stir in the tomato purée, canned tomatoes and stock. Simmer for 25 minutes until reduced and the sauce has thickened.

Stir in the beans, tomato ketchup and chipotle sauce, then cook for 5 minutes. Season well with salt and pepper.

Serve with baked crisp jacket potatoes topped with diced avocado, coriander, dollops of soured cream and a little cheese if you fancy it.

Beef Bourguignon Pies

'Wow!' is the usual response to these pies and they work just as well for a 'posh dinner' as for a jazzed-up mid-week meal. Serve them with buttery new potatoes with chopped parsley and lots of green veg. The pies are also very speedy to make in comparison to a traditional Bourguignon as the steak takes no time to cook.

SERVES 4

1 sheet of ready-rolled puff pastry
1 egg, beaten

For the beef filling
500g rump steak, cut into bite-sized
    chunks
1 onion, chopped
2 tbsp olive oil
400g mushrooms, preferably
    chestnut
2 garlic cloves, chopped
2 tsp plain flour
150ml red wine
200ml beef stock
1 tbsp tomato purée
a good splash of Worcestershire
    sauce
1–2 tsp brown sugar
salt and freshly ground black pepper
1 tbsp chopped parsley

Preheat the oven to 200°C/Gas mark 6.

In a large pan fry the onion in the olive oil until soft – about 2 minutes – then add the mushrooms and garlic and fry for a couple of minutes.

Add the beef and allow to brown on all sides before stirring in the flour. Cook for 2 minutes before pouring in the red wine, stock and tomato purée. Bring to a simmer and allow the sauce to reduce slightly. This will take about 2–3 minutes. Season with Worcestershire sauce, sugar, salt and pepper. Stir in the parsley.

Transfer the mix to individual dishes of about 14 x 9 x 4cm in size. Cut the pastry into four pieces and use one to top each pie, tucking in the edges. Brush the top with egg and sprinkle with black pepper. Make a small hole in the centre.

Bake in the preheated oven for 20 minutes or until the pastry is golden brown, then serve.

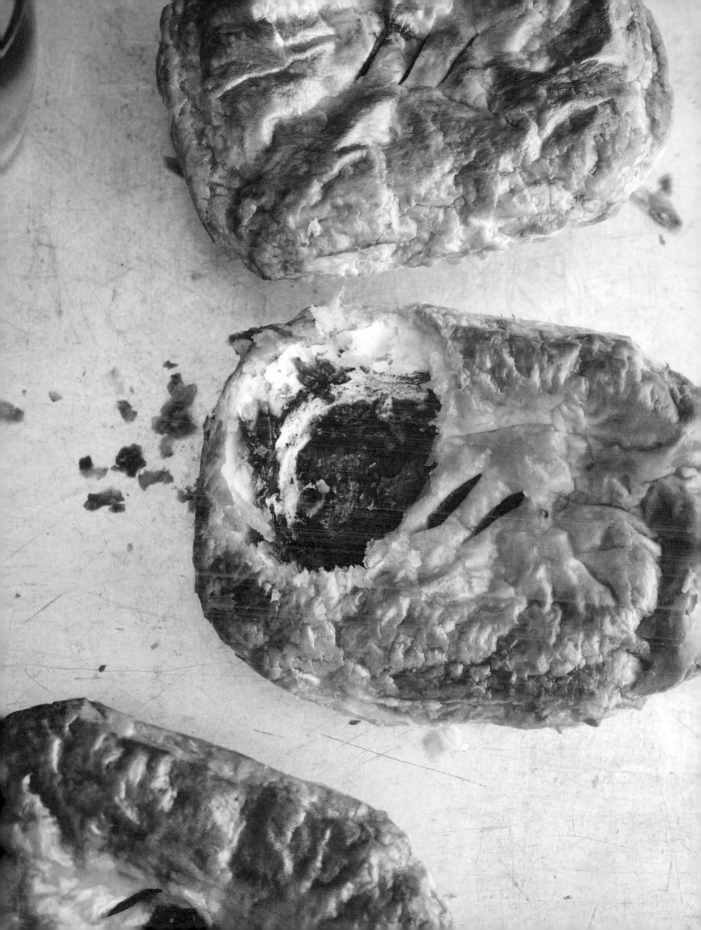

Minute Steak with Pesto, Asparagus and Gnocchi

The clue is in the name – 'minute steak'. Enough said.

SERVES 2

2 x 150g minute steaks, cut into 1cm
  slices
2 tbsp olive oil
150g fine asparagus spears (or green
  beans), cut into 2cm pieces
2 heaped tbsp pesto (home-made
  or shop-bought)
2 tbsp crème fraîche, mascarpone or
  cream cheese
400g shop-bought fresh gnocchi
  (or 175g dried pasta)
1 tbsp finely chopped parsley
salt and freshly ground black pepper

Heat the oil in a frying pan, then quickly fry the steak, no more than 2 minutes. Remove the meat from the pan.

In the same pan fry the asparagus for 2 minutes, then stir in the pesto and crème fraîche.

Meanwhile cook the gnocchi according to packet instructions, then drain, reserving some of the cooking water.

Add the gnocchi to the pan of asparagus along with some of the cooking water to loosen the sauce.

Stir in the cooked steak, parsley and lots of black pepper. Season with salt.

Serve immediately and enjoy.

Steak, Sweet Potato and Avocado Salad

Steak with sweet potatoes is the ultimate comfort dish – you will never want a plain steak again.

SERVES 2

2 x 200g steaks (about 3cm thick),
   whichever is your favourite cut
2 tsp Steak Rub (see page 19)
1 tbsp olive oil
a good cube of unsalted butter

For the sweet potato and avocado salad

200g sweet potato, cut into 1cm
   cubes
1 tbsp olive oil
salt and freshly ground black pepper
1 avocado, sliced
2 large handfuls of salad leaves
2 tbsp pine nuts, toasted

For the dressing

1 tsp Dijon mustard
½ small garlic clove, crushed
1 tbsp balsamic vinegar
3 tbsp olive oil

Preheat the oven to 200°C/Gas mark 6.

To start the salad toss the sweet potato cubes in the oil, season with salt and pepper, then roast in the preheated oven for 25 minutes until soft and slightly caramelised.

Rub the spice mix over both sides of the steaks and fry them in the olive oil and butter for 2 minutes on each side. Leave to rest on a plate for a few minutes, then slice on the angle.

For the dressing mix together the mustard, garlic and balsamic, then add the oil. Season with salt and pepper.

Toss together the roasted sweet potato, avocado, salad leaves and pine nuts. Add the steak slices and dressing and serve.

Slow-roasted Aromatic Beef Brisket

My grandmother Vanda often cooked brisket which if it is cooked very, very slowly – I'm talking about 4–5 hours – becomes super-tender and really delicious. Leftover brisket is great to mince and use as meatballs or stuffed into veg with rice – it's very useful and very Cypriot.

SERVES 6–8

1 x 2kg piece of beef brisket, boned and rolled (don't trim off any fat)
1 tsp freshly grated nutmeg
½ tsp ground cloves
½ tsp ground allspice
2 tbsp freshly ground black pepper
1 tsp ready-chopped ginger
3 tbsp olive oil
3 large onions, cut into thick rings
500ml beef stock
3 tbsp tomato purée
a good glug of red wine
1 tbsp clear honey (optional)

Preheat the oven to 200°C/Gas mark 6.

Mix together the spices on a plate. Rub the beef with a little of the oil and then roll in the spice mix.

Place the onion rings in the bottom of a roasting tray, drizzle with the remaining oil then sit the beef on top. Roast in the preheated oven for 20 minutes.

Remove the beef from the oven and reduce the heat to 140°C/Gas mark 1. Add 100ml of stock then cover the beef and tray with foil. Return to the low oven and slow-roast for 4–5 hours.

Check halfway through and if the onions have started to burn, add a quarter of the remaining stock.

Once cooked and the meat is tender remove from the oven. Remove the meat from the tray and leave to rest, covered with foil.

Push the onions to one side of the tray. Add the tomato purée to the tray and stir well, then pour in a good glug of red wine. Simmer before pouring in the remaining stock and sweetening it with honey if needed. Simmer for 2 minutes and then strain the sauce.

Serve slices of the beef with a little of the sauce and your favourite potatoes.

Curried Roast Beef Wraps

If you are anything like members of my family half the joy of roast beef is the leftovers. Roast beef on Sunday isn't quite the same without a roast beef sandwich of some description the following day. However, you don't have to stick to traditional beef and horseradish – if it's good, anything goes.

MAKES 2 WRAPS

a few slices of leftover roast beef
a pinch of ground cumin
a pinch of ground coriander
1 tbsp olive oil
about 100g leftover roasted veggies
2 soft tortilla wraps
a small handful of spinach leaves

For the curried yoghurt
150ml natural yoghurt
1 tsp curry powder
1 tsp mango chutney
a squeeze of lemon juice
salt

Mix together the yoghurt, curry powder, mango chutney and lemon juice. Season with salt.

Fry the cumin and coriander in the oil for 1 minute then add the roasted vegetables. Cook for a couple of minutes until warmed through.

Cut the beef up into smaller pieces.

Spread a little of the spiced yoghurt on the tortillas in a line down the centre, then top with some of the warmed vegetables, spinach leaves and beef. Fold in the ends and then roll up to create a parcel. Cut in half on the diagonal and serve with the remaining yoghurt.

Beef with Cream and Mushrooms

This recipe is super-quick and can be eaten with mash, rice or pasta. It's a firm favourite in our house and is perfect for when I only have two steaks but need to feed three people – like when an unexpected visitor is invited home after school…

SERVES 2

2 x 200g steaks, rump or sirloin
2 tbsp olive oil
300g mushrooms, chestnut or a
   mixture of different ones, cut into
   chunks
2 garlic cloves, crushed
1 tbsp very finely chopped rosemary
150ml white wine
200ml double cream
1 tbsp wholegrain mustard
salt and freshly ground black pepper

Slice the steak into thin strips.

Heat a frying pan until very hot, then add half the oil. Add the steak and fry for 1 minute. Remove from the pan and set to one side.

Fry the mushrooms in the remaining oil until golden brown and then add the garlic and rosemary. Cook for 1 minute, then pour in the white wine. Simmer until reduced by half.

Add the double cream and mustard. Simmer for a couple of minutes until thickened then add the meat back to the pan to warm through. Season well and serve.

Slow-braised Oxtail with Cinnamon and Rioja

My mother's favourite go-to dish because it reminds her of my Norwegian great-grandma, oxtail is a big hearty dish and I have added plenty of Rioja and orange. The cinnamon adds a warm winter spiciness and everyone loves mopping up the gravy with Paul's crusty seeded bread. This is a dish that tastes even better if cooked up ahead so I sometimes make it on a Saturday afternoon for later in the week.

I usually serve this with a pile of creamy mashed potatoes flavoured with a dollop of horseradish.

SERVES 4–6

1.5kg oxtail pieces
1 tbsp plain flour
salt and freshly ground black pepper
2 tbsp olive oil
2 carrots, cut into chunks
2 onions, sliced
3 celery stalks, cut into chunks
2 garlic cloves, sliced
2 tbsp tomato purée
2 bay leaves
2 cinnamon sticks
1 star anise
500ml Rioja red wine
500ml beef stock
grated zest of 1 orange (or 2–3 tsp redcurrant jelly)

Preheat the oven to 160°C/Gas mark 3.

Season the flour with salt and pepper, then toss the oxtail pieces in this. In a large casserole dish fry the oxtail in batches in the oil until golden brown. Set to one side.

Fry the carrot, onion, celery and garlic in the same dish for 2 minutes before stirring in the tomato purée, bay leaves, cinnamon sticks, star anise and red wine. Bring to the boil then add the oxtail and the stock and stir well.

Cover with a lid and place in the preheated oven for 4 hours.

When the meat is tender carefully remove it from the pan with a slotted spoon then stir in the orange zest (or redcurrant jelly). If the sauce is a little thin simmer it until reduced and slightly thickened. (You could now freeze the meat and its sauce.)

Serve the oxtail with lots of sauce and some creamy mashed potato.

Quick Hungarian Goulash with Paprika

You can throw this together once back from the school run. It tastes even better the next day (better still make a double batch and pop it in the freezer for yet another day).

SERVES 4

600g steak, rump, fillet or sirloin,
    sliced 1cm thick
2 tbsp olive oil
2 onions, sliced
1 tbsp smoked paprika
1 tsp caraway seeds, lightly crushed
1 green pepper, deseeded and cut
    into chunks
1 red pepper, deseeded and cut into
    chunks
1 tbsp tomato purée
200ml beef stock
1 tsp brown sugar
2 tbsp soured cream
finely grated zest and juice of
    1 lemon
salt and freshly ground black pepper

Heat the olive oil in a large pan and fry the onion along with the paprika and caraway seeds for 2 minutes. Add the steak and peppers and fry for 1 minute.

Stir in the tomato purée, stock and sugar. Bring to the boil then simmer for 20 minutes.

Stir through 2 tbsp of soured cream, the lemon juice and zest and season well with salt and pepper.

Minute Steak with Tarragon Butter and Mini Roasties

Just like my dry rubs (see page 19) flavoured butters are a great way to quickly add interest to meat and fish. In this recipe I have made a tarragon butter but you can change this for any other herb or even caramelised shallots, lemon zest or garlic. Make up big batches, roll into a sausage shape in a sheet of clingfilm and pop in the freezer: when it's needed simply slice off a couple of rounds and leave to melt on your cooked meat.

SERVES 2

2 x 150g minute steaks (thickness of
  a £1 coin)
200g new potatoes, cut in half
3 tbsp olive oil
salt and freshly ground black pepper
1 lemon

For the tarragon butter
50g salted butter, softened
1 tbsp chopped tarragon

For the watercress salad
1 tsp Dijon mustard
a squeeze of lemon juice
a squeeze of clear honey
2 tbsp olive oil
2 handfuls of watercress
1 shallot, cut into thin rings

Preheat the oven to 200°C/Gas mark 6.

Boil the new potatoes for 5 minutes then drain. Place in an ovenproof dish, drizzle with some of the oil and season with salt. Use a peeler to peel strips of lemon zest and add these to the dish. Toss everything together, then roast in the preheated oven for 15 minutes until the potatoes are crisp.

Mix together the butter, tarragon and 1 tsp freshly ground black pepper. Chill.

Drizzle the steaks with some oil, season with salt and pepper then fry in a really hot griddle pan for 1 minute on each side for rare/medium-rare. Remove from the pan and leave to rest for a couple of minutes.

Mix together the mustard, lemon juice, honey and olive oil. Then stir through the watercress and shallot rings.

Serve the steaks, sliced on the diagonal, with the roasted new potatoes and watercress salad. Put a dollop of the tarragon butter on top of each serving allowing it to slowly melt.

Lamb

Living in Kent we eat a lot of lamb. It's
perfect roasted with lots of vegetables and
roasties on Sunday but it's also versatile and
great in quick mid-week meals, as chops,
cutlets, mince or as leftovers with veg in
wraps or a quick curry.

When I travelled round Africa and southern
Europe I ate lamb as street food, fragrant
with cumin, coriander and other spices so
I've woven these tastes and experiences into
this chapter. Mid-week dinners will never
be the same again.

Rack of Lamb with Cassis, Redcurrants and Crumbled Chèvre

Racks of lamb can be a little more expensive than other cuts but sometimes I need a mid-week meal that's special. I often cook this for Paul and me when it's just the two of us and a good mid-week catch-up is needed.

SERVES 2

1 x 7-bone rack of lamb, trimmed
1 tsp cumin seeds
1 tsp coriander seeds
1 tsp fennel seeds
2 tbsp olive oil
3 tbsp Cassis
200ml lamb or chicken stock
25g butter
a handful of fresh redcurrants
   (frozen are just as good)
salt and freshly ground black pepper
100g chèvre goat's cheese

Preheat the oven to 200°C/Gas mark 6.

Toast the spices in a dry frying pan, then grind in a pestle and mortar. Mix together with half the olive oil. Rub the spice mix over the lamb.

Fry the lamb on all sides in the remaining olive oil until brown, a few minutes only. Place on a baking tray and pop into the oven for 15 minutes. Once cooked leave the lamb rack to rest for 8 minutes.

Into the frying pan you cooked the lamb in, on a very high heat, pour the Cassis, then the stock. Simmer for 5 minutes until thickened slightly. Remove from the heat, whisk in the butter and stir in the redcurrants. Season with salt and pepper.

Spoon the sauce over the lamb then crumble the goat's cheese on top. Serve with mash or sautéed potatoes.

Asian Red Curry Lamb Broth with Baby Courgettes

I'm not into ready-made sauces but one that can always be found tucked at the back of the fridge is a Thai curry paste. You can easily make your own and it's not difficult but often I don't have all the ingredients so a jar just saves time mid-week when you have hungry mouths to feed.

SERVES 4

650g lamb, leg or shoulder, cut into
  bite-sized pieces
1 tbsp vegetable oil
2 tbsp bought red curry paste
2 lemongrass stalks, bruised with the
  back of a knife
2 x 400ml cans coconut milk
8 baby courgettes, halved lengthways
a handful of frozen peas
1 tsp brown sugar
Thai fish sauce
lime juice

To serve
cooked jasmine rice
lots of coriander leaves
2 tbsp salted peanuts, roughly
  chopped

In a wok heat the oil and fry the curry paste for 2 minutes. Add the lemongrass stalks and lamb and allow the lamb pieces to brown all over.

Pour in the coconut milk and simmer for 20 minutes.

Add the courgettes and cook until tender. Stir in the peas and cook for a couple of minutes.

Season the sauce with brown sugar, Thai fish sauce and lime juice to taste.

Serve on a bed of jasmine rice with a scattering of coriander and peanuts.

Breaded Lamb Cutlets with Cinnamon Apple Sauce

I'm always tweeting about my apple scrumping! I hate to see good apples go to waste and in my last book I gave my super-easy microwave apple-sauce recipe. Apples and lamb are a match made in heaven so here's another way of cooking them but you can mix and match the sauce recipes if you prefer.

SERVES 4

8 lamb chops
125g fresh breadcrumbs
2 tsp chopped thyme leaves
salt and freshly ground black pepper
3 eggs, beaten
2 tbsp olive oil

For the apple sauce
40g butter
2 Bramley apples, peeled
1 eating apple, peeled and finely
    diced
1 tbsp light brown sugar
1 tsp ground cinnamon
juice of ½ lemon

If you want to use my microwave method for apple sauce, go ahead, and just add a dash of cinnamon. Otherwise melt the butter in a saucepan on a medium heat. Grate the Bramley apples into the butter and cook until starting to soften. Then add the diced apple. Stir in the sugar, then add the cinnamon and lemon juice to taste. Add a splash of water to loosen if needed. Set to one side.

When ready to cook the lamb chops mix together the breadcrumbs and thyme. Season the lamb and press down on the eye of the meat to thin it out a little. Dip the chops in the egg followed by the breadcrumbs. Pat down firmly so that they are well coated.

Fry the chops in the olive oil for 3 minutes on each side or until brown.

Serve the chops with your quick apple sauce.

Lamb Leftovers with Harissa Roast Veg and Minted Burritos

I'm a huge fan of tortilla wraps and Josh loves them too. They are so easy to fill! I always have a packet in my freezer for last-minute fajitas and burritos. Who wants to 'faff' around mid-week when we're all hungry, after all?

SERVES 2

2 large soft tortilla wraps

For the filling

200g leftover roast lamb, cut into
   bite-sized pieces
3 tbsp olive oil
1 heaped tbsp harissa paste
grated zest of 1 orange
1 tbsp thyme leaves
salt
1 green pepper, deseeded and cut
   into strips
1 red onion or 4 spring onions, sliced
1 aubergine, cut into chunks
1 sweet potato, cut into small chunks
a few asparagus stalks or green beans
a few cherry tomatoes, halved
2 bay leaves
2 tsp mint jelly

Preheat the oven to 200°C/Gas mark 6.

Mix together 2 tbsp of the olive oil, the harissa, orange zest, thyme leaves and a pinch of salt. Place all the veggies in a roasting dish, pour over the olive oil mix, then toss everything together with the bay leaves. Roast in the preheated oven for 20 minutes until slightly softened.

Fry the lamb in the remaining olive oil until crisp, then stir in the mint jelly and allow to melt.

Wrap the roasted veggies and the crisp minted lamb in tortillas whilst still warm and serve immediately.

Oregano Lamb Skewers with Tomato and Red Pepper Sauce

There is nothing quite like a summer barbecue. Our garden seems to trap all the wonderful smells produced by cooking on coals and when we do get a warm summer's evening, a chilled bottle of wine is opened whilst we sit outside waiting for our delicious supper to cook…

SERVES 4

500g lamb leg meat, cut into 2.5cm cubes
2 red peppers, deseeded and cut into 2.5cm cubes
2 tsp dried oregano
grated zest and juice of 1 lemon
2 tbsp olive oil
2 garlic cloves, sliced
salt and freshly ground black pepper
8 fresh bay leaves

For the sauce
2 shallots, diced
2 tbsp olive oil
2 garlic cloves, sliced
1 red chilli, chopped
400g cherry tomatoes, halved
100ml white wine
1 x 290g jar char-grilled red peppers, drained
a handful of basil leaves

You will need eight bamboo skewers, soaked in water, or eight metal skewers.

Mix together the lamb, peppers, oregano, lemon zest and juice, olive oil and garlic. Season well and leave to marinate for a while if you have time.

For the sauce fry the shallot in a little olive oil for 2 minutes. Add the garlic, chilli and tomatoes and cook until they soften. Pour in the white wine and boil to reduce by half. Add the jarred peppers and warm through. Throw in the basil then blend (best done in a blender rather than using a stick blender) until smooth. Season well with salt and pepper.

Preheat a griddle pan or barbecue.

Thread the meat and peppers on to the skewers, adding a bay leaf in the middle. Cook the kebabs for 3–4 minutes on each side until golden brown outside and pink in the middle.

Serve with the tomato sauce and some boiled rice.

Arabic Lamb Shank with Griddled Pitta Breads

So this isn't my usual super-quick dinner as it does take a while to cook but it's a great recipe for throwing together and bunging in the oven whilst you rush off to collect kids from school. The work is all done for you in the long slow cook and it's the most delicious comfort food to tuck into after a hard day.

SERVES 4

4 lamb shanks, excess fat trimmed
1 tbsp olive oil
1 onion, finely chopped
3 tsp ground cumin
1 tsp ground nutmeg
1 tsp black peppercorns, crushed
1 tsp ground turmeric
1 tsp ground cinnamon
salt and freshly ground black pepper
2 garlic cloves, chopped
4cm piece of fresh root ginger, grated
500ml lamb or chicken stock

To serve
4–6 pitta breads
40g butter
lots of coriander and mint leaves, chopped
about 60g natural yoghurt
2 tbsp pomegranate seeds

Preheat the oven to 150°C/Gas mark 2.

Heat the oil in a deep casserole dish with a lid, and fry the onion until starting to brown. Stir in the cumin, nutmeg, pepper, turmeric, cinnamon and a good pinch of salt.

Add the garlic and ginger, stir, then add the lamb shanks and stock. Cover with the lid and cook in the preheated oven for 3 hours. Once cooked, if the sauce needs reducing simmer on the hob for a few minutes.

Heat a griddle pan. Brush the pitta breads with butter and griddle until blackened lines appear on both sides. Keep warm.

Serve the lamb shanks with lots of fresh coriander and mint, dollops of natural yoghurt, pomegranate seeds and the blackened pitta breads.

Arabic Spiced Lamb Kebabs with Shallot Mayo and Tabbouleh

I love Middle Eastern food and the flavours and textures of this dish put it up there with the best of them! The perfumed richness of the lamb combines perfectly with the sharpness of the shallot mayonnaise and the tomato couscous is so good you could eat it on its own. So make sure there's enough for the following day!

SERVES 4

500g lamb leg meat, cut into 2cm
   cubes
2 tbsp Arabic Spice Mix (see page 16)
2 tbsp olive oil
1 red onion, cut into chunks
salt and freshly ground black pepper

For the shallot mayo
8 tbsp mayonnaise
1 small shallot, finely diced
2 tbsp lemon juice

For the tomato and parsley salad
250g couscous
300ml boiling chicken stock
4 large tomatoes, quartered,
   deseeded and diced
40g parsley leaves, chopped
3 tbsp olive oil
juice of 1 lemon

Marinate the meat in the spice mix and olive oil for 10 minutes or, better still, overnight.

Mix together the mayo, shallot and lemon juice, then season well. Set to one side.

Place the couscous in a large bowl. Pour over the boiling stock, cover with clingfilm and leave to stand for 5 minutes. Fluff the grains with a fork.

Preheat a griddle pan (or a grill).

Thread the lamb on to metal skewers alternating with the separated pieces of red onion. Season with a little salt. Cook the kebabs for 5 minutes on the hot griddle pan turning regularly. Remove from the pan and leave to rest.

Once the couscous has cooled down stir in the tomatoes, parsley, olive oil and lemon juice. Season well.

Serve the kebabs with the tabbouleh and a big dollop of shallot mayo.

Moussaka

A firm family favourite is 'Monday-night moussaka'. We always purchase a larger joint of lamb for slow-roasting on a Sunday just so I can use the leftovers to make my cheat's moussaka. If you don't happen to have any leftover roast lamb, simply brown off some minced lamb and use that instead.

SERVES 4

500g leftover lamb leg or shoulder, cut into small bite-sized pieces
3 tbsp olive oil
2 large aubergines, cut into 2cm cubes
1 onion, chopped
1 tsp ground cinnamon
¼ tsp ground allspice
1 tsp ground coriander
2 garlic cloves, chopped
1 tbsp tomato purée
1 x 400g can chopped tomatoes
1 tbsp sweet chilli sauce
2 tsp dried oregano
2 heaped tbsp chopped mint leaves
salt and freshly ground black pepper

For the topping
2 big dollops of crème fraîche
500ml ready-made good-quality white sauce
2 egg yolks
100g Feta cheese, crumbled
1 heaped tbsp Parmesan cheese, grated

Preheat the oven to 200°C/Gas mark 6.

Heat the oil in a large frying pan, then fry the diced aubergine until softened. Remove from the pan and set to one side.

In the same pan fry the onion until soft and translucent, then stir in the spices and garlic. Cook for 1 minute.

Add the lamb and tomato purée and stir well. Throw in the canned tomatoes, sweet chilli sauce and herbs, then simmer for 10 minutes. Season well with salt and pepper.

For the topping mix together the crème fraîche, white sauce and egg yolks.

Layer the meat and aubergines in a 20 x 25cm ovenproof dish: lamb, aubergine, lamb, aubergine, lamb. Pour over the white sauce mix and then sprinkle with the Feta or Parmesan.

Bake in the preheated oven for 15 minutes or until golden brown and serve with a big green salad.

Peas   Flour
Ham   Butter
Eggs   Lamb
Milk   Chicken
Spinach   Pork sausages
Pine nuts   Caster Sugar
Plums.

Lamb and Lentil Curry

There is nothing quite like the smell of toasted spices. Once you have a good selection to hand you can mix and match to achieve different flavours – hot and spicy or aromatically fragrant. The cardamom pods in this dish have a spicy citrus flavour that complements the lamb perfectly. I have used canned lentils instead of dried because I like it quick… quick… quick for that Monday to Friday meal!

SERVES 4

500g lamb steaks, cut into 2cm cubes
25g butter
1 tbsp olive oil
1 onion, sliced
2 garlic cloves, chopped
2 cardamom pods, seeds only
1 tsp black mustard seeds
½ tsp chilli powder
½ tsp ground turmeric
1 tsp ground cumin
1 tsp ground coriander
1 tsp tomato purée
2 x 400g cans chopped tomatoes
1 x 400g can cooked lentils
2 tsp garam masala
2 tbsp Greek yoghurt
salt

To serve
pitta or naan breads
lots of coriander leaves

Heat the butter and oil in a large pan and fry the onion, garlic and spices for 2 minutes then add the lamb. Stir well to coat the lamb in the spices, then add the tomato purée, canned tomatoes and a splash of water. Simmer for 25 minutes.

Stir in the lentils, garam masala and Greek yoghurt, season with salt and warm through. (Freeze when chilled if desired.)

Serve with pitta or naan bread and lots of fresh coriander.

Moroccan Lamb with Apricots

This is a long slow cook of a recipe. It's the sort of thing that you need to be a little bit organised for but there is a trade-off. Get it ready before the school run, throw it in the oven and by the time you are back from football practice supper is ready. The other bonus is that leftovers freeze really well. So one small bit of forethought and you have meals ready for tonight and next week.

SERVES 8

2kg lamb neck fillet, cut into 3cm
    chunks
1 tbsp plain flour
3 tbsp olive oil
2 onions, sliced
3 garlic cloves, sliced
1 tbsp ground coriander
1 tbsp ground cumin
2 tsp ground allspice
½ tsp chilli powder
a large pinch of saffron strands
2 large cinnamon sticks
1 x 400g can chopped tomatoes
a little clear honey
200g dried apricots
salt and freshly ground black pepper
pomegranate seeds (optional)

To serve
steamed couscous
2 tbsp roughly chopped nuts
    (almonds, pistachios, pine nuts,
    walnuts or hazelnuts, optional)
lots of coriander leaves

Preheat the oven to 160°C/Gas mark 3.

Coat the lamb in flour then, in a casserole dish, fry in batches in a little oil until brown. Then remove from the pan.

Fry the onions until soft in a little more oil, then throw in the garlic, coriander, cumin, allspice and chilli. Add the meat back to the pan along with the saffron, cinnamon sticks, tomatoes, honey, apricots and 1 litre cold water.

Bring to the boil, cover, then place in the oven for 2½ hours or until the meat is tender. Season well. Sprinkle with pomegranate seeds (optional).

Serve with couscous, nuts (if using) and lots of fresh coriander.

Stilton Lamb Chops with Mango Salsa

I love the combination of savoury flavours with sweet fruits, especially where cheese is involved. This recipe might sound a bit strange but trust me it works and is just the thing to brighten up a dull Monday!

SERVES 4

8 lamb chops
50g Stilton cheese
a few mint leaves, chopped
1 tbsp olive oil
salt and freshly ground black pepper

For the mango salsa
1 large mango, diced
1 small red onion, finely chopped
grated zest and juice of ½ orange
a pinch of chilli flakes
2 spring onions, chopped
2 tbsp olive oil

For the salsa mix together the mango, onion, orange zest, chilli and spring onions. Whisk together the oil and orange juice. Season this with salt and pepper. Keep both separate for now.

Preheat the grill.

Roughly mash together the Stilton and mint.

Drizzle the chops with oil and season then grill for 2–3 minutes on each side. Once browned top each one with some of the Stilton mix and grill for a further 2 minutes to melt the cheese.

Dress the mango and onion mixture with the oil and orange juice.

Serve the chops with the mango salsa, perhaps with some new potatoes and a green salad.

Fish is big in our house. My son almost prefers it to meat
and therefore it's on our table at least twice a week if not
more. It's quick to cook and very versatile: if pushed for
time you can just shove it in the oven with a few vegetables
and a little seasoning and it pretty much cooks itself in no
time at all. If your family are not seafood fans start them
off on my Baked Crab and Coconut Cakes with sweet chilli
mayo – you'll soon have them hooked!

Don't be afraid of cooking fish: there's really not much to
it and the results are mouthwateringly worthwhile!

Fish

Super Simple Fish Supper

This is lush and healthy, a winner in my book!

SERVES 2

2 tbsp olive oil
2 x 150g pieces of cod, haddock or any white fish, skin off, boned
2 tsp Greek Island Herb Mix (see page 15)
100g cherry tomatoes, halved
1 tbsp capers, drained
a few pitted black olives, halved
a few cooked baby new potatoes, halved
a splash of ouzo (optional)
1 lemon
1 tbsp roughly chopped parsley

Preheat the oven to 180°C/Gas mark 4.

Cut two squares of foil about 30 x 40cm and drizzle one side of each piece with a little of the olive oil.

Dividing your ingredients between the two foil sheets place a piece of fish on each then sprinkle over your Greek Island Herb Mix. Scatter with the cherry tomatoes, capers, olives and new potatoes, then drizzle with a little more olive oil. Fold the foil over the fish to make a parcel but leaving a little gap at the top to add a splash of ouzo, then close.

Place both parcels on a baking tray and bake in the preheated oven for 20 minutes.

Once cooked remove from the oven and carefully open the parcels – watch out for the steam. Remove the fish and veg to warmed plates, squeeze over a little lemon juice and scatter with chopped parsley. Serve immediately.

Soul Fish

My mum makes a variation of this and when Josh was little and we went to stay at Grandma's, this was his supper of choice. He called it 'soul fish' and I couldn't agree more – this sole is definitely soul food in my book!

SERVES 2

4 sole fillets, skin on
1 tbsp plain flour
1 tsp ground cumin
salt and freshly ground black pepper
1 tbsp olive oil
a knob of butter
a few sprigs of dill
1 tbsp capers, drained

For the tomato sauce

1 garlic clove, sliced
1 tbsp olive oil
a splash of red wine if you have it
    around
1 x 400g can cherry tomatoes
a small handful of basil leaves, torn
a pinch of sugar
a small dash of red wine vinegar
a handful of pitted black olives,
    halved

For the tomato sauce, in a medium pan fry the garlic in the oil until golden. Pour in the wine followed by the tomatoes and basil leaves.

Simmer slowly for 15 minutes, then season with sugar and vinegar, salt and pepper, then stir in the olives. Allow to warm through.

Mix together the flour and cumin and season well with salt and pepper. Lightly coat the fish in the flour then fry, skin-side down, in the hot olive oil and butter for 3 minutes before turning over and cooking for 1 minute on the other side.

Add the dill and capers to the pan, heat through briefly, then serve the fish with the rich tomato sauce.

Coquilles St 'Fish Pie' Potatoes

This is another of those 'Twitter' recipes that was created from bits of salmon left over from the previous night's drinks party and a lone packet of scallops in my freezer – and it's just lush! I'm a firm believer in using up what you already have in your fridge. My mother's favourite saying was 'waste not, want not' and this recipe proves you can magic something great out of leftovers. Try using king prawns or white fish in this or a handful of cooked frozen peas and lardons mixed with the fish is pretty tasty too…

SERVES 4

4 baking potatoes
40g Parmesan cheese, grated
25g fresh breadcrumbs

For the fishy filling
40g butter
35g plain flour
350ml milk
1 tbsp wholegrain mustard
2 tbsp chopped chives
200g scallops, either large ones, quartered, or small Peruvian
100g smoked salmon, chopped, or trimmings
1 tbsp vodka or Pernod
salt and freshly ground black pepper

Preheat the oven to 180°C/Gas mark 4.

Stab the potatoes with a fork then put in the oven for 1¼ hours or until soft in the centre.

To start the filling melt the butter in a pan then stir in the flour. Cook for 2 minutes then gradually whisk in the milk. Bring to the boil stirring all the time. Stir in the mustard, chives and fish with a splash of vodka, and cook for 2 minutes. Season well and set to one side.

When the potatoes are cooked cut in half and scoop out the middle (leaving a border of potato). Roughly mash the potato flesh. Mix this together with the fish mixture.

Spoon this fish and potato mixture back into the potato skins then sprinkle over the Parmesan and breadcrumbs. Bake for a further 10–15 minutes until golden brown and hot through, then serve.

Salmon and Asparagus en Croûte

This recipe is straight out of *The Good Life*, being just the sort of thing glorious Margot would cook for Gerry whilst wearing a frilled hostess-gown – I love that 70s vibe! It's super-easy and absolutely delicious. If you don't have asparagus to hand try it with wilted spinach instead.

The pieces of salmon need to be a similar shape and thickness all the way through. And if you want a sauce with it make a hollandaise or try reducing some fresh fish stock (bought supermarket is fine) with a little double cream or crème fraîche and a squeeze of lemon juice.

SERVES 4

2 x 250g blocks of puff pastry
1 egg, beaten

For the salmon
2 x 500g pieces of salmon fillet,
   pin-boned and skinned
225g asparagus, woody ends
   removed
150g cream cheese
grated zest of 2 lemons
2 tbsp chopped dill
1 tbsp wholegrain mustard
salt and freshly ground black pepper

Preheat the oven to 200°C/Gas mark 6. Line a baking tray with greaseproof paper.

Blanch the asparagus in boiling water for a couple of minutes, then drain and cool. Pat dry with kitchen paper.

Mix together the cream cheese, lemon zest, dill and mustard. Season well. Spread the cream-cheese mixture over the top of one salmon fillet. Place the asparagus spears on top spreading them out evenly. Cover the asparagus with the other piece of salmon. Season.

Roll the pastry out until it is as thick as a £1 coin. Cut it into two.

Place one piece of pastry on the lined baking tray then place the salmon 'sandwich' in the middle. Brush the edges of the pastry with beaten egg, then top with the other piece of pastry. Press the edges down firmly and crimp. Brush the whole thing with egg, decorating the top with any pastry off-cuts.

Bake in the preheated oven for 25–30 minutes until golden brown. Test if it is cooked by inserting a skewer into the centre for 10 seconds: pull it out and, if warm, the salmon will be medium; if hot, it will be well done.

'Black Bomber' Bake

It's time to get the image of stodgy student tuna pasta bake out of your heads. This is a comforting pasta dish with an oozy, bubbling cheese sauce made with our favourite Cheddar cheese, Black Bomber. It's perfect for mid-week when you have forgotten to buy fresh fish.

SERVES 4

400g dried short pasta (penne, rigatoni etc.)
50g butter
40g plain flour
500ml milk
1 tsp Dijon mustard
100g rocket leaves, roughly chopped
250g strong Cheddar cheese, grated
2 x 120g cans tuna in oil, drained
1 x 200g can sweetcorn, drained
salt and freshly ground black pepper
3 tbsp fresh breadcrumbs

Preheat the oven to 180°C/Gas mark 4.

Cook the pasta according to the packet instructions but reduce the time by 1½ minutes. Drain, reserving 3 tbsp of the pasta cooking water.

Melt the butter in a large saucepan. Add the flour and cook for 2 minutes. Slowly whisk in the milk and bring to the boil stirring all the time.

Once boiled remove the roux from the heat, then stir in the mustard, rocket and cheese (reserving a large handful). Stir until the cheese has melted. Stir through the pasta, reserved pasta water, tuna and sweetcorn. Season well with salt and pepper.

Tip into an ovenproof dish, sprinkle over the breadcrumbs and remaining cheese. Bake in the preheated oven for 10 minutes until bubbling and golden brown.

Stir-fried Curry Prawns

On school nights if you are ever really short of time stir-fries are the thing to cook as they are super-quick. I sometimes cheat and buy a bag of stir-fry veg so there is even less prep to do. I love adding a bit of curry powder – think Singapore noodles here, as it adds wonderful warmth – and it's a bit different to the sweeter Chinese stir-fries.

SERVES 4

250g raw king prawns
1 onion, sliced
3 tbsp vegetable oil
2 garlic cloves, chopped
5cm piece of fresh root ginger, grated
2 tsp hot curry powder
1 red pepper, deseeded and sliced
1 large carrot, cut into thin rounds
a handful of sugar-snap peas
a handful of tenderstem broccoli, cut into 2cm pieces
200g fine egg noodles
3 tbsp soy sauce
2 tbsp oyster sauce

To serve
lots of coriander leaves
lime wedges

In a wok fry the onion in a little of the oil for 1 minute. Add the prawns, garlic, ginger and curry powder. Fry until the prawns turn pink then tip out on to a plate.

In the same wok, in a little more oil fry the pepper, carrot, sugar-snaps and broccoli until tender.

Meanwhile cook the egg noodles following packet instructions until tender and then drain. Toss in the remaining oil.

Add the cooked prawns, noodles, soy sauce and oyster sauce to the wok. Toss everything together until hot.

Serve in bowls with tons of fresh coriander and a wedge of lime.

Asian Cod

If I am really organised I throw this together in the morning and leave it to marinate in the fridge all day. But if you are running out the door and have not been able to do that, then even just 10 minutes in the marinade helps the cod absorb all the Asian flavours.

SERVES 2

2 x 200g pieces of cod, skin on,
   or frozen cod fillets
5cm piece of fresh root ginger,
   chopped
2 garlic cloves, sliced
1 red chilli, chopped
1 tbsp clear honey
1 tsp Chinese five-spice powder
3 tbsp light soy sauce

To serve
100g sticky rice
2 heads of pak-choi, quartered
2 tsp sesame oil
1 tbsp sesame seeds, toasted
juice of 1 lime

In an ovenproof dish mix together the ginger, garlic, chilli, honey, five-spice powder and soy. Add the cod and coat well in the sauce. Leave to marinate if you have time.

Preheat the oven to 200°C/Gas mark 6.

Add a little water or stock to the ovenproof dish, then bake the cod in the preheated oven for 15–20 minutes or until cooked through.

Meanwhile cook the sticky rice following packet instructions. Stir-fry the pak-choi in the sesame oil for a few minutes.

Once the cod is cooked serve on a bed of the sticky rice with the stir-fried pak-choi and a sprinkling of sesame seeds and lime juice.

Baked Rainbow Trout with Ras-el-hanout and Peppers

This is a very simple but extraordinarily tasty dish. Ras-el-hanout is a North African spice mix with rose petals, mace, coriander, nutmeg and clove which is perfect for baked fish. The flavour is reminiscent of the street food you find in the medinas and markets in Morocco and Tunisia.

SERVES 2

2 rainbow trout, gutted and scaled
1 small orange, cut into rounds
a few sprigs of thyme
1 tbsp ras-el-hanout
3 tbsp olive oil
salt and freshly ground black pepper
1 red pepper, deseeded and cut into strips
1 yellow pepper, deseeded and cut into strips
1 garlic clove, thinly sliced
1 lemon, cut into chunks

Preheat the oven to 190°C/Gas mark 5.

Make four cuts in the skin on both sides of each trout. Stuff the cavity of the trout with orange slices and thyme. Place the fish in an ovenproof dish.

Mix together the ras-el-hanout and 2 tbsp of the olive oil. Brush over the skin of the fish using it all up. Season with a little salt.

Place the pepper strips, garlic slices and lemon chunks around the fish. Drizzle with the remaining oil then season with salt and pepper.

Bake in the preheated oven for 20 minutes depending on the size of the fish. Serve with couscous and natural yoghurt or crème fraîche.

Salmon with Mascarpone, Cheddar and Horseradish Crust

If you have fussy kids salmon is a good fish to get them started. It's not strong in flavour and it's really good for you. The horseradish gives this a bit of warmth and spice.

SERVES 4

4 x 200g salmon fillets, skin on, scaled and pin-boned
6 tbsp mascarpone cheese
2 tbsp horseradish sauce
salt and freshly ground black pepper
40g fresh breadcrumbs
1 tbsp chopped herbs (dill, parsley and/or thyme)
50g Cheddar cheese, grated

Preheat the oven to 200°C/Gas mark 6.

Place the salmon fillets in a baking dish skin-side down.

Mix together the mascarpone and horseradish and season well with salt and pepper. Spread this mixture on top of the fillets.

Mix together the breadcrumbs, herbs and cheese. Season well, then scatter over the mascarpone on top of the fillets.

Place the baking dish in the preheated oven and bake the salmon for 15 minutes.

Serve with sautéed potatoes and greens.

Prawn and Chicken Jambalaya

Sometimes I just want a meal that we can eat while curled up together on the sofa. Warming, spiced comfort food in a bowl that is perfect to eat with a fork whilst putting the world to rights.

SERVES 4

1 tbsp olive oil
1 onion, chopped
2 peppers (any colour), deseeded and diced
150g cooking chorizo, sliced
2 garlic cloves, chopped
2 celery stalks, diced
2 tsp Cajun Spice Mix (see page 19)
1 tbsp tomato purée
200g arborio risotto rice, or long-grain rice
about 500ml chicken stock
200g cooked chicken, diced
200g cooked prawns
30g butter
a squeeze of lemon
salt and freshly ground black pepper

To garnish
a pinch of sweet smoked paprika
4 spring onions, sliced

Heat the oil in a heavy pan and fry the onion, peppers, chorizo, garlic and celery until translucent.

Add the spice mix, tomato purée and rice and stir well. Pour in a cup of chicken stock, stir then allow to simmer until absorbed, then add another cup. Keep going until the rice is cooked 'al dente'.

Stir in the cooked chicken and prawns and a final splash of stock. Stir in the butter and a squeeze of lemon. Season.

Serve with a sprinkling of paprika and chopped spring onion.

Baked Crab and Coconut Cakes

When we were younger my sister and I used to go crabbing then cook and devour what we caught. I still love going to Margate today to eat fresh crab on the harbour wall – a delicious 'kiss-me-quick' treat… So here is my alternative mid-week-dinner crab recipe.

SERVES 4

300g white crabmeat
3cm piece of fresh root ginger, grated
2 red chillies, finely chopped
1 tbsp finely chopped coriander
3 eggs
salt and freshly ground black pepper
100g fresh breadcrumbs
4 tbsp desiccated coconut
3 tbsp plain flour
about 2 tbsp vegetable oil

For the sweet chilli mayo
6 tbsp mayonnaise
2 tbsp sweet chilli sauce
juice of ½ lime

In a large bowl mix together the crabmeat, ginger, chilli, coriander, one of the eggs, a pinch of salt and 50g of the breadcrumbs.

Shape this mixture into eight patties. Chill in the fridge for 10 minutes (you can freeze them at this point).

Mix together the mayonnaise, sweet chilli and lime juice and place in a serving bowl.

Preheat the oven to 180°C/Gas mark 4.

Mix together the remaining breadcrumbs and the coconut. Beat the remaining two eggs. Put the flour on a plate. Dip the cakes first in the flour, then the egg, then the breadcrumb mixture.

Fry the cakes in oil until golden brown – a couple of minutes on each side – then place on a baking tray and bake in the preheated oven for 5–10 minutes until hot.

Serve the crab cakes with the sweet chilli mayo.

Meat-free

Meat-free dinners are often seen as options for vegetarians only but they don't have to be: they can be just as filling and as interesting as their meaty cousins. Gone are the days where every meat-free dish is either a mushroom risotto or a stuffed pepper.

From meat-free curries to spicy Spanish eggs you really can adapt many of your favourite meat dishes into something where vegetables are the star. If your household is anything like ours we often have lots of veggies in the fridge and leftover cooked ones from the night before. There might be little or no meat as the supermarket shop has just had to wait, so making a quick simple dinner with your leftovers is the obvious choice!

Aubergine Curry

My style of cooking means that you can get every ingredient in a big supermarket but one ingredient that can be difficult to find but I love to use is fresh curry leaves. Although you can buy them dried, the fresh ones have a much better flavour. You might have to go to an Asian supermarket or sometimes the big supermarkets have them near the fresh herbs. But once you have got your hands on them buy a few packets and pop them in the freezer ready for another day.

SERVES 4

3 large aubergines, cut into 2cm
    cubes
3 tbsp olive oil
4 cardamom pods, lightly crushed
2 tsp ground cumin
1 tsp black mustard seeds
2 garlic cloves, crushed
5cm piece of fresh root ginger,
    grated
2 tsp garam masala
a handful of curry leaves (optional)
a small bunch of coriander,
    including the stalks
2 x 400g cans chopped tomatoes
a pinch of sugar, if needed
salt

To serve
mini pitta breads, grilled
sweet mango chutney
6 dollops of natural yoghurt

In a large frying pan fry the aubergine cubes in batches in a little olive oil until golden brown. Remove each batch, drain on kitchen paper and set to one side.

In the same pan fry the cardamom, cumin and mustard seeds, garlic, ginger and garam masala for a minute.

Add the curry leaves and aubergine to the pan along with the stalks of the coriander that have been very finely chopped. Mix everything together before pouring in the tomatoes.

Bring to a simmer and cook for 5 minutes, then season with salt and a pinch of sugar if needed.

Serve the curry with the coriander leaves, pitta bread, mango chutney and a dollop of yoghurt.

Beetroot, Feta and Mint Risotto

If you love beetroot then this is the dish for you. It is rare to get a dish as colourful as this – it just brightens my mood. It turns the most amazing pink colour but take care not to stain the entire kitchen and all your utensils as I have done in the past!

SERVES 4

400g cooked beetroot
1 onion, finely chopped
1 large garlic clove, chopped
2 tbsp olive oil, plus a little extra
75g butter
375g arborio risotto rice
150ml white wine
about 1 litre vegetable stock, hot
50g Parmesan cheese
1 tbsp mint chopped, plus a few
   extra leaves to serve
salt and freshly ground black pepper
grated zest of 1 lemon
100g Feta cheese

Blitz half the beetroot to a fine purée. Cut the remaining beetroot into 1cm cubes.

Fry the onion and garlic in 2 tbsp of the oil and 25g of the butter until soft and translucent, about 2 minutes. Add the rice and fry for another 2 minutes coating it in the oil.

Pour in the white wine and stir all the time until it is completely absorbed.

One ladle at a time, add the stock, stirring continuously, allowing each ladleful to be absorbed before adding the next one. This should take about 16 minutes. Halfway through stir in the puréed beetroot and beetroot cubes.

Once the rice is cooked but still has a bite remove from the heat. Add one last ladleful of stock along with the Parmesan, the remaining butter and the mint. Stir well, season and leave to stand for 30 seconds.

Serve in warm bowls topped with a drizzle of extra olive oil, the grated lemon zest, crumbled Feta and a few mint leaves.

Paneer Coconut Curry

Paneer – a fresh Indian cheese – is a great alternative to meat and I often have a block or two in my fridge. I love using it as it soaks up all the spices in the sauce and even my die-hard meat-eating husband tucks in when he comes home for a curry dinner.

SERVES 4

1 large onion, chopped
2 tbsp olive oil
a knob of butter
5cm piece of fresh root ginger, grated
2 garlic cloves, chopped
2 tsp garam masala
2 tsp ground turmeric
1 tbsp curry powder
1 tsp ground cumin
2 x 400g cans chopped tomatoes
500g paneer, cut into cubes
1 x 400ml can coconut milk
salt and freshly ground black pepper
a large handful of frozen peas

To serve
a handful of cashew nuts (optional)
cooked basmati rice
small bunch of coriander, chopped
2 naan breads, halved

Fry the onion in the olive oil and butter until translucent. Add the ginger, garlic, garam masala, turmeric, curry powder and cumin. Stir well before pouring in the chopped tomatoes and half a can of water (measured using the tomato can). Simmer gently.

Fry the paneer in a dry frying pan until golden then transfer to the curry sauce.

Stir in the coconut milk and simmer for 8–10 minutes.

Season well before stirring through the peas, then cook for 2 minutes.

Dry-fry the cashew nuts until golden, then serve the curry on a bed of rice with a handful of chopped coriander and the toasted cashew nuts. Serve with naan bread.

Paprika-spiced Vegetable Frittata

You can quite easily use up any leftover veggies in this recipe. I often have honey-roasted parsnips leftover from a Sunday lunch as well as cooked carrots and green beans. You can basically use whatever you want and that goes for the cheese as well. Comté, Cheddar, goat's cheese or Gruyère all work well and the more you add the more oozy it gets.

SERVES 2–4

1 red onion, sliced
2 red peppers, deseeded and sliced
2 tbsp olive oil
350g asparagus, woody ends
   removed, then cut into 2cm pieces
225g cooked new potatoes, halved
2 tsp smoked paprika
6 eggs, beaten
salt and freshly ground black pepper
50g Feta cheese
50g Cheddar cheese, grated

Preheat the grill.

Fry the onion and peppers in the olive oil until soft (a 23cm non-stick frying pan should do the trick). Then add the asparagus and potatoes. Fry until warmed through then stir in the paprika. Cook for 1 minute.

Season the eggs and then pour over the vegetables. Stir and cook on the hob for 8–10 minutes or until the eggs are just set. Take care not to burn the bottom.

Crumble over the Feta and sprinkle over the Cheddar, then pop under the grill until golden brown. Serve in big wedges with a green salad.

Rainbow Stir-fry with Pak-choi and Cashew Nuts

There's nothing like a simple stir-fry for a supper in a hurry. Anything and everything can go into it, which fits my cooking ethos down to the ground. I like to keep simple sauce ingredients such as soy, sweet chilli, oyster sauce and sesame oil in the cupboard and fridge ready and waiting for a quick mid-week dinner.

SERVES 4

1 tsp cornflour
2 tbsp light soy sauce
5cm piece of fresh root ginger, minced
2 garlic cloves, chopped
2 tbsp sweet chilli sauce
2 tbsp oyster sauce
2 tbsp sesame oil
1 red onion, sliced
2 carrots, peeled with a peeler into ribbons
200g green beans
150g baby corn
1 head of pak-choi
2 peppers, deseeded and sliced
a good handful of shredded red cabbage
1 red chilli, chopped
1 x 225g can water chestnuts, drained
40g cashew nuts

To serve
cooked jasmine rice or plain rice
lime wedges
sesame seeds

Mix together the cornflour and 1 tbsp of water in a small bowl. Add the soy sauce, ginger, garlic, sweet chilli and oyster sauces. Mix well and set to one side.

Heat the sesame oil in a wok. Stir-fry the veg including the water chestnuts, until starting to soften, then push everything to one side. Pour the sauce in, then stir everything together, adding in the cashew nuts.

Serve with rice, a wedge of lime and a sprinkling of sesame seeds.

Spicy Vegetable Fritters with Lime Yoghurt Dip

Use up any leftover veg for this recipe. I like to use squash, pepper, asparagus, new potatoes, onions and green beans but you can also try aubergine, courgettes and even canned sweetcorn if it needs bulking out a little bit. It's ready in minutes and is completely satisfying.

SERVES 2

250g cooked vegetables
2 eggs, beaten
a small bunch of coriander, chopped
  (keep some to garnish)
1 tsp ground turmeric
1 tsp hot chilli sauce or chilli flakes
4 spring onions, chopped
2 heaped tbsp plain flour
salt and freshly ground black pepper
2–3 tbsp olive oil

For the lime yoghurt dip
150ml natural yoghurt
grated zest and juice of 1 lime

Chop up the cooked veg and place in a mixing bowl. Add the eggs, coriander, turmeric, chilli sauce, spring onions and flour. Season with salt and pepper. Mix well until you have a loose batter consistency.

Heat a little oil in a frying pan. When hot fry spoonfuls of the mixture pressing them down slightly for a couple of minutes on both sides.

Mix together the yoghurt, lime juice and zest. Season well.

Serve the fritters with a scattering of coriander leaves and the lime yoghurt. It's as simple as that.

Potato Wedges with Garlicky Tomato Ketchup

Finger-lickin' food at its best. I cook the potato wedges in duck fat but if you don't like duck fat, try olive oil instead. This is a super-quick supper at its best!

SERVES 4

4 large Maris Piper potatoes, scrubbed and cut into wedges
1 tbsp plain flour
salt and freshly ground black pepper
1 tbsp chopped oregano or rosemary
2 good spoonfuls of duck fat (or goose fat or olive oil)
2 garlic cloves, in their skins

To serve
4 tbsp tomato ketchup
a good dash of Tabasco or chilli sauce
a small block of Feta cheese, crumbled
a few basil leaves, torn

Preheat the oven to 200°C/Gas mark 6.

Par-boil the potato wedges for 4 minutes, then drain. Season the flour, add the oregano, then toss the wedges in this.

Put the duck fat into a roasting tray and heat through in the oven. Add the potato wedges and garlic cloves, toss together and then roast until golden brown and crisp, about 25 minutes.

Mix together the tomato ketchup and Tabasco. When the garlic is soft remove it from the roasting tray. Squeeze the flesh from the skins and crush this with a fork. Stir into the ketchup mix.

Serve the potato wedges in a bowl with the crumbled Feta, torn basil leaves and black pepper, and the garlic and chilli tomato ketchup.

Puy Lentil, Beetroot and Sage Salad

I can remember when cooking with lentils came into fashion in the 1970s. My mother would have split orange lentils in the cupboard, which would be thrown into soups to bulk them out. At the time they seemed very exotic but they took an age to cook and needed soaking the night before. These days, after spending years in France, nutty Puy lentils are my favourite. I often have a packet of cooked Puy lentils in the cupboard for speedy suppers but dried ones these days take only 20 minutes to cook.

SERVES 4

250g dried Puy lentils
250g cooked beetroot, cut into 2cm
   chunks
3 tbsp olive oil
8 sage leaves
2 tbsp balsamic vinegar
1 tbsp clear honey
2 large handfuls of rocket leaves
2 shallots, cut into thin rings
2 tbsp hazelnuts, roasted and
   roughly chopped
100g goat's cheese

Rinse the Puy lentils, then cook according to the packet instructions. Alternatively buy pre-cooked lentils. Drain and rinse well.

Fry the beetroot in a little oil to warm through. Tear in the sage, fry for 1 minute then add the balsamic vinegar and honey. Leave to cool slightly.

Mix together the lentils, rocket, shallots and hazelnuts.

Add the cooled beetroot to the lentil mixture along with the dressing made in the frying pan.

Crumble over the goat's cheese and serve.

Spanish Eggs

This is another of my dad's favourites. It is an easy scrumptious dinner for two but also when toast and marmalade won't cut it and a fry-up just isn't right, this recipe makes the most wonderful weekend brunch as well.

SERVES 2

4 spring onions, chopped
1 yellow pepper, deseeded and diced
1 green pepper, deseeded and diced
2 tbsp olive oil
1 tsp paprika
½ tsp chilli flakes
1 x 400g can chopped tomatoes
a few basil leaves, torn
a splash of balsamic vinegar
salt and freshly ground black pepper
4 large eggs
50g Manchego cheese, grated, or
   any other good hard cheese
2 tbsp crème fraîche
1 tbsp chopped parsley

Preheat the oven to 190°C/Gas mark 5.

In a large pan fry the spring onions and peppers in olive oil until soft, then stir in the paprika and chilli flakes. Pour in the canned tomatoes. Bring to a simmer then stir in the basil and a splash of balsamic vinegar. Allow to reduce slightly, then season well.

Pour into two 15cm shallow dishes or a large ovenproof dish. Make two 'wells' in the tomato sauce in each dish and crack an egg into each one. Sprinkle with cheese.

Stand the dishes in a shallow tray of water then bake for 10–15 minutes or until the egg whites are cooked through and the yolks are runny.

When cooked remove the dishes from the water. Add some dollops of crème fraîche, season the tops of the eggs and sprinkle with parsley. Serve with warm crusty bread.

Pasta

Well, who doesn't love pasta? It's so versatile, you can make a quick mid-week meal out of odds and ends. My cupboard is always stuffed with packets of rigatoni, fusilli and linguine, all ready for my next creation!

There are some really quick recipes here but I want you to use them more for ideas. They are not to be followed word for word but used as inspiration so you can make the recipes work for you. You can add and take away many of the ingredients so that they fit in with what you have lurking in the fridge.

One tip though: when cooking pasta drain it and reserve a little of its cooking water. This is great for loosening the sauce and because the water is full of starch, it will give it a silky finish. It sounds a little 'cheffy' but it's what every Italian does.

Leftover Veggie Pasta with Crumbled Roquefort and Croûtons

Please use this as a rough idea for a recipe. If you don't have leftover roasted veggies in the fridge from last night don't panic. You can either roast some or fry off quick-cooking ones like courgettes, peas and spinach. This is simply my 'go-to' recipe when there is a handful of leftover veggies but not enough to make a good soup.

SERVES 2

150g short pasta, such as penne
salt and freshly ground black pepper
any leftover roasted vegetables, such
    as butternut squash, peppers,
    onion and aubergine
1 tbsp olive oil
1 tbsp thyme leaves
3 tbsp ricotta cheese
grated zest of 1 lemon
100g Roquefort cheese

For the croûtons
2 slices of sourdough bread
1 tbsp olive oil

For the croûtons brush the sourdough slices with oil, cut into squares then pan-fry until crisp. Set to one side.

Cook the pasta in lightly salted boiling water according to the packet instructions. Drain whilst reserving a little of the cooking water.

Fry the roasted veggies in olive oil until warmed through. Then add the thyme leaves.

Remove from the heat and stir through the ricotta and lemon zest. Add the pasta and the reserved water to loosen everything. Crumble in three-quarters of the Roquefort and stir. Season with black pepper.

Serve in warm bowls with the remaining crumbled Roquefort and the croûtons on top.

Super-quick Sausage Ragù

Sausages are perfect for making a quick sauce to go with pasta. They have already been seasoned so are full of flavour and take minutes to cook. I like the ones my local farm shop makes with a little chilli but any good-quality ones will do perfectly!

SERVES 4

300g pasta
salt and freshly ground black pepper
1 tbsp olive oil
8 good-quality sausages, skins
   removed
2 leeks, halved and sliced
1 tbsp chopped sage
a good splash of white wine
200ml chicken stock
100g crème fraîche
Parmesan shavings
chopped parsley

Cook the pasta in lightly salted boiling water according to the packet instructions. Drain whilst reserving about 3 tbsp of the pasta cooking water.

Heat the olive oil in a frying pan. Break up the sausage meat into the pan and fry, breaking it up further with a wooden spoon, until golden brown.

Add the leeks and sage, then reduce the heat and fry until soft.

Add the wine then bubble until it has almost disappeared. Pour in the stock and then stir in the crème fraîche. Season.

Stir together the pasta and sauce loosening it with the pasta water (as required), then serve sprinkled with Parmesan shavings and chopped parsley.

Scallops 'Mami Cola'

This was a bit of a 'Twitter hit' based on my godmother Monique's mum's recipe and it uses one of my favourite ingredients – scallops. It's not for every day but sometimes even mid-week suppers need to be special.

SERVES 2

150g linguine pasta
salt and freshly ground black pepper
2 tbsp olive oil
100g saucisson, thinly sliced
2 garlic cloves, thinly sliced
1 red chilli, chopped
6 large scallops, about 180g meat, chopped
4 tomatoes, quartered, deseeded and diced
grated zest of ½ lemon
1 tbsp chopped chives

Cook the linguine in lightly salted boiling water according to the packet instructions. Drain whilst reserving a little of the cooking water.

Meanwhile heat the oil in a frying pan and fry the saucisson for a couple of minutes, then add the garlic and chilli. Cook for 1 minute more.

Push everything to one side then add the scallops. Fry for 30 seconds then flip over.

Add the tomatoes, pasta and a little cooking water to the pan and stir.

Season well, stir in the lemon zest and chives, then serve.

Cheat's Tortilla Lasagna

Lasagna is one of those dishes that however hard you try to recreate somebody else's recipe it never tastes the same as when they cook it. It can be just as good but it will always be different. This is my cheat's version for when you are busy and don't have time to make a two-hour meat sauce, a white sauce and then cook it for 45 minutes.

SERVES 3–4

4 soft tortilla wraps, wholemeal or
  plain
50g Cheddar cheese, grated

For the meat sauce
500g minced beef
2 tbsp olive oil
1 onion, finely chopped
1 large carrot, grated
2 garlic cloves, chopped
a good splash of red wine
250g mushrooms, sliced
1 tbsp tomato purée
2 tsp dried oregano
1 x 400g can chopped tomatoes
150ml beef stock
salt and freshly ground black pepper

For the 'white sauce'
200ml crème fraîche
80g Parmesan cheese, grated
a pinch of ground nutmeg

Heat the olive oil in a large pan and fry the onion and carrot until translucent. Add the garlic and minced beef breaking it up with a wooden spoon. Fry until browned.

Pour in the red wine and bring to the boil before stirring in the mushrooms, tomato purée, oregano, tomatoes and stock. Stir well and simmer for 10 minutes until reduced. Season.

Preheat the oven to 200°C/Gas mark 6. Grease a shallow casserole dish or lasagna dish about 20cm round.

Mix together the crème fraîche, Parmesan and nutmeg. Season.

Spoon a little of the beef into the bottom of the dish (about 3 tbsp), then top with two tortilla wraps. Spoon half the remaining beef on top then dollop over half of the crème fraîche mix. Top with two tortillas, then the remaining beef followed by the remaining crème fraîche mix.

Sprinkle over the Cheddar cheese and bake in the oven for 10 minutes or until the cheese has melted and become golden brown. Serve.

Bacon and Basil Pasta

This is quick, quick, quick… Instead of a smooth traditional tomato sauce the tomatoes are left chunky and are just warmed through. It reminds me of pasta dishes in Italy where the cherry tomatoes are so full of flavour they are like sweets.

SERVES 4

300g pasta
salt and freshly ground black pepper
200g smoked bacon lardons
1 tbsp olive oil
2 garlic cloves, thinly sliced
1 red chilli, chopped
400g cherry tomatoes, halved
a splash of white wine
about 2 tbsp torn basil leaves
Parmesan shavings

Cook the pasta in lightly salted boiling water according to the packet instructions. Drain whilst reserving a little of the cooking water.

In a medium pan fry the bacon in olive oil until crisp, then drain off some of the excess fat. Add the garlic and chilli and stir before throwing in the tomatoes. Cook for 1 minute.

Add the wine, bring to a simmer then stir in the pasta and half the basil. Season well before serving with Parmesan shavings and the remaining basil leaves.

Garlicky Seafood Pasta

Another big 'hit' with my son and it's not for the faint-hearted – the garlic is pretty pungent!

SERVES 4

300g of your favourite long pasta, spaghetti, tagliatelle etc.
salt and freshly ground black pepper
6 garlic cloves, thinly sliced
3 tbsp olive oil
a good splash of white wine
1 tbsp good-quality balsamic vinegar
1 x 400g can chopped tomatoes
200g seafood mix
200g prawns, peeled
200g squid rings
a handful of basil leaves

Cook the pasta in lightly salted boiling water according to the packet instructions. Drain whilst reserving about 3 tbsp of the pasta cooking water.

In a large pan fry the garlic in olive oil until starting to turn lightly golden brown then add the wine. Stir in the balsamic vinegar and tomatoes and a splash of water. Simmer for a few minutes.

Add the seafood to the pan and cook until the prawns are pink.

Stir through the basil leaves and pasta, loosening the sauce if needed with the reserved pasta water. Season well and serve.

Pasta Chicken Bake

I love pasta bakes and there is often a fight around the table as to who gets all the crunchy bits from around the edges of the dish. As long as you under-boil the pasta and then keep the sauce loose you shouldn't end up with a stodgy dish but a creamy pasta with a perfectly delicious crunchy topping.

SERVES 4

300g short pasta, e.g. fusilli
salt and freshly ground black pepper
1 tbsp olive oil
3 chicken breasts, skinned and cut
  into bite-sized chunks
1 garlic clove, crushed
4 spring onions chopped
200g mushrooms, quartered
2 tbsp flour
150ml white wine
500ml chicken stock
200ml double cream
a large handful of frozen peas
2 tbsp chopped tarragon

For the topping
50g Parmesan cheese, grated
25g fresh breadcrumbs
2 tbsp chopped parsley

Preheat the oven to 200°C/Gas mark 6.

Cook the pasta in lightly salted boiling water for 1½ minutes less than the packet states. Drain, reserving 150ml of the cooking water.

Heat the olive oil in a large pan and fry the chicken until lightly brown. Add the garlic, spring onions then the mushrooms and fry for 2 minutes. Stir in the flour and cook for another minute.

Pour in the white wine and bubble until reduced by half. Add the stock and cream, bring to a simmer, then throw in the peas, tarragon and pasta. Mix everything together. Season well.

You want the sauce to be loose so that the bake does not go stodgy in the oven. You can loosen it with the reserved pasta water. Now pour the pasta into a 20 x 25cm ovenproof dish.

Mix together the Parmesan, breadcrumbs and parsley. Scatter over the top of the pasta. Bake in the oven for 10 minutes or until golden brown and crunchy and serve.

Pasta with Chicken, Spinach, Smoked Paprika and Mascarpone

I love paprika and smoked paprika works a treat with the mascarpone and spinach in this simple dish.

SERVES 2

150g pasta
salt and freshly ground black pepper
100–150g cooked chicken, cut into
  bite-sized pieces
1 tbsp olive oil
1 tsp smoked paprika
200ml tomato passata
2 large handfuls of baby spinach
  leaves
2 big dollops of mascarpone cheese
Parmesan shavings

Cook the pasta in lightly salted boiling water according to the packet instructions. Drain whilst reserving a little of the cooking water.

Fry the chicken in olive oil for 1 minute with the smoked paprika then pour in the passata. Bring to a simmer then stir in the spinach allowing it to wilt, followed by the mascarpone. Season well.

Add the pasta to the sauce, loosening it with a little pasta cooking water if needed. Check seasoning before serving with Parmesan shavings.

Toasties

For those of us that can remember the delight of owning a
toastie machine you will also remember never getting bored
of the novelty of buttering the outside of the bread so that it
went nice and crisp. This chapter is all about taking the plain
old ham and cheese toastie to the next level with grilled toasties,
eggy bread toasties and luxury cheese on toast for the days you
have to get a quick dinner thrown together in minutes: think
'footie' match night and after-school clubs!

Guinness Toasties with Cheddar, Ham and English Mustard

This needs no introduction…

MAKES 1

2 thick slices of good-quality white
  bread, ideally a little stale
50g Cheddar cheese, grated
2 thick slices of ham
1 tsp English mustard
1 egg, beaten
2 tbsp Guinness
salt and freshly ground black pepper
a knob of butter
1 tbsp olive oil

Make a simple cheese and ham sandwich with a little English mustard.

Beat the egg and Guinness together, then season.

Dip the sandwich into the egg mixture allowing it to absorb the egg.

In a frying pan, heat the butter and oil over a medium heat. Fry the egg-dipped sandwich until golden brown, turning the heat down so that it cooks long enough for the cheese inside to melt.

Once cooked remove from the pan, drain on kitchen paper if necessary and serve.

Mushrooms on Toast with Cranberry Glaze

Another leftover Christmas favourite because you can never have too much cranberry!

SERVES 1

3 flat-cup or Portobello mushrooms
a little butter
salt and freshly ground black pepper
1 thick slice of sourdough bread
1 tbsp grated Gruyère cheese
1 tbsp cranberry jelly
green salad leaves, to serve

Fry the whole mushrooms in a little butter and season well.

Preheat the grill and toast the sourdough on both sides.

Place the mushrooms on top of the sourdough, then top with grated Gruyère. Place under the grill until melted.

Warm the cranberry jelly with a splash of water to loosen it to a runny consistency.

When the Gruyère has melted serve the mushroom toast with green salad leaves and a drizzle of the cranberry glaze.

Ciabatta Bread Pizzas

These are my go-to meal for a school-night supper or a quick bite before footie… and you can pile on whatever your team prefers: meat, pineapple, chorizo, any cheese you fancy. So go on, load 'em up high and dish 'em out!

SERVES 2

2 small ciabatta breads, cut in half horizontally
salt and freshly ground black pepper

For the quick tomato sauce
300g cherry tomatoes, halved
a pinch of chilli flakes
1 tbsp olive oil
a pinch of caster sugar (optional)

For the toppings
ham or Parma ham, with olives, anchovies, capers or mushrooms – anything goes
2 small handfuls of grated mozzarella or Cheddar
2 tbsp Italian Herb Mix (see page 16)
3 tbsp freshly grated Parmesan

Preheat the oven to 180°C/Gas mark 4.

For the tomato sauce cook the halved tomatoes and chilli flakes in the olive oil over a medium heat, stirring occasionally, allowing the tomatoes to break down. Once you have a thick chunky sauce remove from the heat. Add salt and pepper to taste and a pinch of sugar if needed.

Place the four pieces of ciabatta, cut-sides up, on a baking tray. Divide the tomato sauce between them and spread out.

Top with your favourite topping (or toppings), then sprinkle over the cheese. Finally sprinkle over the Italian Herb Mix and the Parmesan. Place in the preheated oven and bake for 10 minutes or until the cheese has melted and turned a golden brown. Serve immediately with a fresh crunchy salad.

Maple Bacon and Fried Egg on Toast

Very naughty, very indulgent – but oh so good…

SERVES 1

4 rashers of maple-cured streaky
  bacon
2 eggs
a splash of milk
1 thick slice of white bread
a little olive oil
a knob of butter
maple syrup, to serve

Grill the bacon until crisp.

Whisk together one of the eggs and a splash of milk. Dip the bread in the egg mixture allowing it to soak some of it up.

Fry the bread in a little oil and butter until golden brown. Fry the other egg in the same pan.

Serve the eggy bread with crisp bacon, the fried egg and a little maple syrup.

Grilled Sourdough, Chocolate, Brie and Basil

I spotted this on TV and tried it. It's sooo delicious, it had to go in my book. It's a cross between a snack supper and a pudding. LUSH!

SERVES 1

1 thick slice of sourdough bread
a little olive oil
a few slices of ripe Brie, at room
  temperature
a little 80% dark chocolate
a few basil leaves

Brush the sourdough with olive oil, then toast both sides on a hot griddle pan.

Whilst the bread is still hot top with Brie. Grate over a little dark chocolate then scatter with fresh basil leaves. Finish with a drizzle of olive oil and serve.

Bacon, Beetroot and Beaufort Triple Decker

A blissful dinner for one…

SERVES 1

4 pieces of maple-cured bacon
3 medium slices of bread
2 cooked beetroot, sliced
1 large gherkin, sliced
50g Beaufort cheese, grated
  (if you can't find Beaufort,
  try Camembert)

Grill the bacon.

Toast the bread on one side under the grill.

Take two pieces of the bread. Top the untoasted side of one with bacon and beetroot, and the other with gherkin and cheese. Put one on top of the other, fillings up, and top with the other slice of toasted bread, untoasted side down.

Secure the layers with a cocktail stick, then cut into two chunky triangles.

Red Onion Marmalade, Cream Cheese and Turkey Toastie

Usually saved for post Christmas and I often add in any lurking stuffing and vegetables. It's perfect when you just want a light supper.

SERVES 1

2 slices of good-quality multigrain bread
1 tsp soft butter
a little cream cheese
1 tbsp red onion marmalade
a few slices of cooked turkey (or chicken)

Get your toasted sandwich maker nice and hot.

Butter the bread slices on one side only, then turn them over.

Spread one unbuttered side with cream cheese, dot with onion marmalade then layer on the turkey.

Top with the other piece of bread (butter on the outside), then toast in your machine until golden and crisp. Serve hot.

French Toast with Mozzarella, Pesto and Rocket

Josh's favourite Saturday snack supper. I make it in my paella pan if he has his friends round and I have a big batch to make.

MAKES 1

2 thick slices of good-quality granary bread, ideally a little stale
1 ball of mozzarella, drained and sliced
a handful of rocket leaves
1 tbsp pesto
1 egg, beaten
a splash of milk
1 tbsp chopped chives
salt and freshly ground black pepper
a knob of butter
1 tbsp olive oil

Make a sandwich with the mozzarella, rocket and pesto.

Beat together the egg and milk, then add the chives, salt and pepper.

Dip the sandwich into the egg mixture allowing it to absorb the egg.

Heat the butter and oil over a medium heat. Fry the egg-dipped sandwich until golden brown, turning the heat down so that it cooks long enough for the cheese inside to melt.

Once cooked remove from the pan, drain on kitchen paper if necessary and serve.

Grilled Goat's Cheese on Toast with Rocket and Sweet Red Onion

This is a take on a favourite dish I always order when I visit my childhood friend Honor in the south of France. She has a beautiful farmhouse gite just a stone's throw from the Canal du Midi where a friend of hers has a tiny restaurant on the quayside, serving food on rickety tables in the sunshine. The flavours of the sharp goat's cheese and the sweetness of the red onion transport me straight back to my seat in the sun. Perfection!

SERVES 2

2 large slices of sourdough bread
1 tbsp olive oil
1 garlic clove
2 individual goat's cheese rounds
1 tsp Provençal Herb Mix (see page 15)
a large handful of rocket leaves
a few walnut halves, roughly chopped

For the sweet red onion
1 red onion, finely sliced
1 tbsp olive oil
2 tsp brown sugar
1 tsp red wine vinegar

For the sweet red onion fry the onion in the olive oil until softened, about 2 minutes. Sprinkle in the brown sugar and stir well. Add the vinegar and bubble for a couple of minutes until sticky. Set to one side ready for later.

Preheat the grill.

Brush both sides of the sourdough bread with the olive oil then grill until golden brown. Rub one side of each slice with the garlic clove.

Cut each cheese in half through the middle giving you four rounds in all. Sprinkle the cut side with your herb mix, then place two rounds on each piece of toast.

Place under the grill for a couple of minutes or until the cheese starts to melt.

Once the cheese is oozy remove from the grill. Top the cheese on each toast with the sweet red onion, the rocket leaves and walnut pieces and serve warm.

Smoked Salmon, Dill and Horseradish

My grandmother's sandwich of choice with all the Norwegian flavours she loved.

SERVES 1

1 heaped tbsp crème fraîche
a dollop of horseradish sauce
freshly ground black pepper
2 slices of rye bread
a few slices of smoked salmon
a little fennel bulb, finely sliced/
    shaved
grated zest and juice of 1 lemon
a few fronds of dill

Mix together the crème fraîche and horseradish. Season well with pepper.

Toast the rye bread on both sides, then spread with a little crème fraîche mixture. Top with smoked salmon, fennel shavings and lemon zest and juice. Top with a further dollop of crème fraîche and some dill, then serve.

Something Sweet

I'm not big on mid-week puddings but sometimes we all need something sweet to finish the day with. Although you don't want to 'faff' around with a fiddly recipe you probably have all the ingredients you need sitting in your cupboard. So it's just a case of going to have a look at what you have and using a little imagination, like my Baked Apple Crunch. Don't forget your leftovers either. Some day-old teacakes or croissants can be substituted for the brioche in the White Chocolate and Raspberry Brioche Pudding or use up that white loaf that's been hanging around the bread-bin a day too long. No fresh fruit? Never mind, bring out the canned peaches or apricots, it will all taste delicious!

Pears with Ginger and Mascarpone Cream

Pears with ginger – a marriage made in heaven…

SERVES 4

40g caster sugar
40g butter
a glug of brandy
3 pears, peeled, cored and cut into
    8 wedges each
grated zest of 1 lemon
2 balls of stem ginger, finely chopped
    or grated
150g mascarpone cheese
1 vanilla pod or 1 tsp vanilla bean
    paste
1–2 tbsp icing sugar
a few ginger-nut biscuits (optional)

Sprinkle the sugar over the base of a frying pan. Heat gently and allow it to caramelise. Add the butter then stir in the brandy.

Add the pears and lemon zest. Cook gently until the pears are warm and soft.

Mix together the ginger, mascarpone, vanilla and icing sugar.

Serve the warm pears with a drizzle of their buttery juices and a good dollop of mascarpone cream. If you like bash up some ginger-nut biscuits and sprinkle over.

No-bake Cheesecake Pots

These little pots of goodness are the perfect way to clear out your fridge, biscuit tin and fruit bowl all in one go. You can make them as naughty as you want and adapt the recipe to whatever you have lying around.

SERVES 4

200g soft fruits (blueberries, raspberries, strawberries)
3 tbsp icing sugar
a splash of Amaretto (optional)
200g mascarpone or cream cheese
½ tsp vanilla extract or vanilla bean paste
200ml Greek yoghurt or any other yoghurt you have in the fridge, including fruit ones
12 amaretti biscuits or 8 digestive biscuits, crushed
2 tbsp granola (optional)

Place the fruits in a bowl and sprinkle over 1 tbsp of the icing sugar and a splash of Amaretto. Mix and leave to stand for 10 minutes.

Mix together the mascarpone, vanilla and the remaining 2 tbsp of icing sugar. Fold in the yoghurt and set to one side.

Take four glasses and add crushed biscuits to the base. Spoon the mascarpone mixture on top. When ready to serve spoon over the fruit mixture. Finally if you have a little granola in the cupboard sprinkle this over the top and serve.

Spiced Cherry and Chocolate Turnovers

I always have a packet of puff pastry in my fridge. It is just so versatile for both sweet and savoury dishes. This recipe also uses canned fruit. As long as you get it in natural juices it's a perfect store-cupboard ingredient especially when a fruit is out of season. The turnovers also freeze beautifully, but make sure you wrap them individually (before drizzling with chocolate) and pop them in a freezer-proof box.

SERVES 4

1 ready-rolled sheet of puff pastry
1 egg, beaten
75g dark chocolate, whatever you
    have in the cupboard

For the filling
400g canned pitted cherries, drained
    and halved
1 tbsp caster sugar
grated zest of 1 orange
¼ tsp ground cinnamon
a pinch of grated nutmeg
2 tbsp cherry or raspberry jam

For the filling cook the cherries, sugar, orange zest, cinnamon and nutmeg for 5 minutes on a low heat in a medium pan. Stir in the cherry jam and bring to a simmer. Once it is thick and syrupy, remove from the heat and leave to cool.

Preheat the oven to 180°C/Gas mark 4.

Cut the pastry into eight squares and place on a baking sheet. Put a spoonful of cherry mixture in the middle of each square. Brush the edges with egg, then fold one pastry side over to create a triangular parcel. Press down the edges to seal. Brush with beaten egg and make a little cut in the top.

Bake the parcels for 10–15 minutes or until golden brown and oozy.

Whilst they are cooking melt the chocolate.

Once the turnovers are cooked remove from the oven and leave to cool slightly before drizzling over the melted dark chocolate. Serve warm.

Nutella, Pear and Granola Quesadillas

I know it is naughty but Nutella is one of those things that sits in the back of the cupboard for a while and then when you need a chocolate kick it appears, ready to save the day. It is a great ingredient when you are short of time as it replaces the need to melt chocolate: you can simply scoop it out of the jar and get going.

SERVES 2

2 soft tortilla wraps
1 tsp soft butter
1 tsp caster sugar
2 tbsp Nutella
1 ripe pear, cored and thinly sliced
2 tbsp granola

Lay the tortilla wraps on the work surface. Brush a little butter on one side of each wrap. Then dust with a little sugar.

Turn one wrap over and spread the other side with the Nutella. Place the thin slices of pear on top – no need to peel – and sprinkle with granola. Top with the other tortilla wrap so that the sugared side is facing outwards.

Fry on both sides in a dry frying pan for 1–2 minutes or until golden brown, then serve plain or with vanilla ice-cream.

Baked Apple Crunch

Baked apples are never going to be the Cindy Crawford of puddings, they just don't look that pretty. However, as we all know looks can be deceiving and this is certainly the case with this recipe. A show-stopper it is not, but its combination of sweet filling and slightly tart apple is a real winner.

SERVES 4

4 eating apples
50g butter
3 tbsp clear honey
a handful of dried cranberries, dried cherries or raisins
1 tsp ground cinnamon

Preheat the oven to 180°C/Gas mark 4.

Core the apples then place in an ovenproof dish.

Melt the butter and honey together, then stir in the dried cranberries, cinnamon and crushed-up biscuits. Mix well, then stuff into the cored-out centre of each apple. Sprinkle over any remaining mixture and squeeze over the orange juice.

6 ginger-nut or digestive biscuits,
   crushed into small pieces
juice of 1 small orange
about 250g ready-made custard or
   canned custard
a good slosh of double cream

Place in the preheated oven and bake for
20 minutes.

Warm the custard together with a good slosh
of cream (it's a cheat's posh custard).

Serve the apples with the custard, not forgetting
to drizzle over any of the juices from the dish.

Choccy Bananas

These are so simple and a perfect way of using up those dodgy bananas in
the fruit bowl. Traditionally we do this dessert on the embers of a summer
barbecue but considering we always have bananas and dark chocolate in the
house they are the perfect choccy treat during the week whatever the season.

SERVES 4

4 bananas, unpeeled
75g chocolate, broken into chunks
grated zest of 1 orange
a splash of brandy, for the adults
25g flaked almonds or nuts of
   your choice, toasted and roughly
   chopped

Preheat the oven to 180°C/Gas mark 4.

Make a long slit through the skin of each
banana, then push any chocolate chunks you
have loitering around into the cut.

Place each banana on a piece of foil and grate
over a little orange zest. For adults, this is the
time to add a splash of brandy to each banana
too. Make a parcel with the foil.

Place the foil parcels on a baking sheet and bake
for 15–20 minutes.

Once cooked remove from the oven or barbecue,
carefully unwrap, then sprinkle over a few flaked
almonds for a bit of crunch.

White Chocolate and Raspberry Brioche Pudding

We always have white chocolate buttons in the cupboard (unless Josh has scoffed them!) and thanks to being married to a baker, brioche! But this loaf can stale quite quickly. When it does don't throw it away as it is your secret weapon when making this yummy indulgent pudding. Because of its high butter content there is no need to butter the bread in my take on bread-and-butter pudding.

SERVES 4–6

3 large eggs
300ml double cream
300ml crème fraîche
a little vanilla extract
100ml milk
1 tbsp caster sugar
1 x 600g brioche loaf
120g white chocolate buttons (you can use dark or milk instead)
around 300g raspberries

Preheat the oven to 170°C/Gas mark 3.

Lightly whisk the eggs, cream, crème fraîche, milk, caster sugar and vanilla together.

Cut the brioche into 2cm chunks and scatter half into a buttered 30 x 20cm ovenproof dish along with half the chocolate buttons and raspberries. Repeat this once more.

Pour over the cream and egg mixture, press down lightly then bake for 25–30 minutes or until golden brown. If the chocolate starts to burn reduce the heat a little.

Once cooked remove from the oven and serve warm with cream or custard.

Salted Banoffee Crunchie Eton Pie

This pudding needs no introduction. Just read the title and you'll want to make it!

SERVES 6–8,
depending on your glasses

1 x 397g can condensed milk
   caramel
500g cream cheese
200ml double cream, lightly
   whipped
4 bananas, peeled and chopped
1 tsp vanilla extract
2 Crunchie bars
2 digestive biscuits
a pinch of sea salt

In a large bowl mix together the cream cheese, cream, half the condensed milk caramel, the chopped bananas and vanilla extract. Crush one of the Crunchie bars and mix in as well. Then spoon into wide glasses (tumblers or martini glasses).

Crush together the digestives and the other Crunchie bar, then sprinkle on top of the glasses. Mix together the remaining caramel and the salt then drizzle on top.

Index

horseradish: salmon with mascarpone, Cheddar and horseradish crust 171
smoked salmon, dill and horseradish 228
Hungarian goulash with paprika 128

I
Italian herb mix 16

J
jambalaya: prawn and chicken jambalaya 172
Jewish chicken soup 34

K
kebabs: Arabic spiced lamb kebabs 145
Cypriot pork kebabs with onions and lemon 92
oregano lamb skewers 140
quick tandoori chicken skewers 40
keftedes 87
kidney beans: chilli bean Bolognese 115
pork burritos with kidney beans and cheese 78

L
lamb: Arabic lamb shank with griddled pitta breads 142
Arabic spiced lamb kebabs with shallot mayo and tabbouleh 145
Asian red curry lamb broth with baby courgettes 137
breaded lamb cutlets with cinnamon apple sauce 138
keftedes 87
lamb and cinnamon toastie with quick tomato relish 83
lamb and lentil curry 149
lamb leftovers with harissa, roast veg and minted burritos 139
Moroccan lamb with apricots 150
moussaka 146
oregano lamb skewers with tomato and red pepper sauce 140
Persian lamb with mint, lime and spinach 70
rack of lamb with Cassis, redcurrants and crumbled chèvre 134

Stilton lamb chops with mango salsa 152
stuffed marrow with spicy minced lamb and Feta crumble 79
lamb's lettuce: flat-iron Parmesan steak with lamb's lettuce 112
lasagne: cheat's tortilla lasagne 201
lavender: Provençal mix 15
leeks: Savoyard vegetable soup with Petit Tomme 28
lemons: Cypriot pork kebabs with onions and lemon 92
garlic-stuffed roast chicken with lemon, thyme and honey glaze 63
lemon chicken schnitzel with poached egg and anchovies 49
lemon, coriander and cucumber yoghurt 92
lentils: lamb and lentil curry 149
puy lentil, beetroot and sage salad 190
limes: avocado and lime salad 53
lime yoghurt dip 186
Persian lamb with mint, lime and spinach 70

M
mango salsa 152
maple bacon and fried egg on toast 219
marmalade and balsamic chicken 51
marrows: stuffed marrow with spicy minced lamb and Feta crumble 79
mascarpone: no-bake cheesecake pots 234
pasta with chicken, spinach, smoked paprika and mascarpone 209
pears with ginger and mascarpone cream 233
salmon with mascarpone, Cheddar and horseradish crust 171
meatballs: Cypriot meatballs 87
Swedish meatballs 84
Thai-spiced turkey meatballs with noodles and coconut broth 88
minestrone soup 35
mint: beetroot, Feta and mint risotto 181
comforting pea and ham soup with a hint of mint 32
mint and yoghurt sauce 40
Persian lamb with mint, lime and spinach 70

Acknowledgements

A huge thank you to everyone who has helped me with this, my second book.

To my agent Borra Garson who believed in me and gave me this chance. To the lovely Jan Croxon, for being there, on the end of the phone and not minding when I had a wobbly moment. To my mother and sister for being a constant source of foodie ideas and cups of tea in the garden. To my gaggle of fabulous girlfriends who all had something to say about my book.

Thank you to the team at Hodder & Stoughton – Nicky Ross, Alice Moore, Kate Miles, Emma Knight, Ruth Ferrier – for your friendship and your patience. To the uber talented Dan Jones photographer extraordinaire and to Holly Bruce for prop styling. To Lizzie Harris and Gee Charman, my home economists.

And finally to my husband Paul, for his constant support and sound advice and to my son Josh who waited patiently whilst I photographed and fiddled with meals before I served them up. I love you both so much. X

First published in Great Britain in 2017 by Hodder & Stoughton
An Hachette UK company

1

Copyright © Alex Hollywood 2017
Photography by Dan Jones

The right of Alex Hollywood to be identified as the Author of the Work has been asserted by her in accordance with the Copyright, Designs and Patents Act 1988.

All rights reserved. No part of this publication may be reproduced, stored in a retrieval system, or transmitted, in any form or by any means without the prior written permission of the publisher, nor be otherwise circulated in any form of binding or cover other than that in which it is published and without a similar condition being imposed on the subsequent purchaser.

A CIP catalogue record for this title is available from the British Library

Hardback ISBN 978 1 444 79923 1
Ebook ISBN 978 1 444 79925 5

Editorial Director: Nicky Ross
Editor: Susan Fleming
Project Editor: Kate Miles
Design & Art Direction: Alice Moore
Photographer: Dan Jones
Food Styling: Gee Charman and Lizzie Harris
Food styling assistants: Tamara Vos and Leonie Sooke
Props Styling: Holly Bruce
Shoot Producer: Ruth Ferrier
Proofreader: Margaret Gilbey
Indexer: Caroline Wilding

Printed and bound in China by C&C Offset Printing Co., Ltd.

Hodder & Stoughton policy is to use papers that are natural, renewable and recyclable products and made from wood grown in sustainable forests. The logging and manufacturing processes are expected to conform to the environmental regulations of the country of origin.

Hodder & Stoughton Ltd
Carmelite House
50 Victoria Embankment
London EC4Y 0DZ
www.hodder.co.uk